# Workplace Ethics

# Workplace Ethics

## Winning the Integrity Revolution

**Ralph W. Clark**
**Alice Darnell Lattal**

Rowman & Littlefield Publishers, Inc.

ROWMAN & LITTLEFIELD PUBLISHERS, INC.

Published in the United States of America
by Rowman & Littlefield Publishers, Inc.
4720 Boston Way, Lanham, Maryland 20706

Copyright © 1993 by Rowman & Littlefield Publishers, Inc.

British Cataloging in Publication Information Available


**Library of Congress Cataloging-in-Publication Data**


Clark, Ralph W.
Workplace ethics : winning the integrity revolution /
Ralph W. Clark, Alice Darnell Lattal.
p.    cm.
1.  Business ethics. I. Lattal, Alice Darnell. II. Title.
III. Title: Work place ethics.
HF5387.C55   1992b     174'.4—dc20        92-21386       CIP
ISBN 0-8476-7789-3  (cloth : alk. paper)


Printed in the United States of America

The paper used in this publication meets the minimum requirements of
American National Standard for Information Sciences—Permanence of
Paper for Printed Library Materials, ANSI Z39.48–1984.

Dedicated to:

Ashley, Eric, Jeff, Matthew, Rachel, and Tom
—and the workplaces of their future

# Contents

# Preface

Everyone in business wants to be successful. Most want to be ethical. But far too many people believe that to get ahead in business, one must cut corners. Recent developments in the fields of business management and organizational psychology have helped to close the gap between ethics and success in the workplace. In this book, we demonstrate that ethics and success can be brought even closer together. Our approach is interdisciplinary, drawing upon philosophy, business management, and psychology. We bring together three different stories:

1. The story told by moral philosophy: Do what is right for its own sake. The decision-making model we use for answering difficult ethical questions is "moral pluralism," which entails a commitment to the basic values of rights, justice, the common good, and (when properly balanced against the other values) self-interest.

2. The story told by the current "quality movement" in business: Manage everything—the motivations of workers, relations with suppliers, attention to the needs of customers—so as to produce high-quality goods and services. Treat people well as you strive to run a more competitive business. We show how the quality movement can benefit from input provided by both philosophers and psychologists.

3. The story told by behavioral psychologists who say that coercive, negative styles of personal interaction are harmful: Replace coercion in business with a system of positive expectations

and reinforcements. This story complements advice from the quality movement—to "banish fear from the workplace." It also complements the basic values of moral philosophy. Moreover, the discipline of behavioral psychology stands alone in providing tried and true techniques for achieving behavior change. Such change can help to make the workplace more ethical and more productive.

We say *why* individuals in the workplace ought to treat people well, and we explain *how* to get individuals in the workplace to change so that they will treat people well.

# Acknowledgments

We wish to thank a number of individuals who read and advised us of their reactions to *Workplace Ethics* during various stages of development. We owe them an especially large debt. Those who helped us shape our ideas—to whom we also owe a great debt—are too numerous to list. They include teachers, clients, colleagues, students, and authors. On occasion, we have been influenced by the acts of strangers—salespeople, business owners, secretaries, telephone operators, airline personnel, repair people, and many others. By acting ethically, they helped to demonstrate the power of workplace ethics. They helped to shape our view of what is possible.

Marshall Hammer read the entire manuscript painstakingly; nearly every page is better because of his meticulous and thoughtful editing. The entire book has benefited as well from Theodore Drange's careful reading. Christopher Wheaton and Suzanne Clark read early versions of the book. Their advice assisted us in finding our direction. Andy Lattal gave us invaluable assistance on matters pertaining to psychological theory. Cindy Ashworth and Matthew Lattal provided helpful comments on a number of chapters.

We have had the good fortune to work with a very responsive editor, Jon Sisk, and his editorial staff, in particular Lynn Gemmell, at Rowman & Littlefield.

Needless to say, none of these individuals bears responsibility for any problems that remain.

# Introduction

Actions at work affect us in countless ways. The products and services upon which we depend, the communities in which we live, the well-being of our families, our economic security—all are affected by what happens in the workplace. The kinds of people we are—our commitments to one another, how we view competition and cooperation, our sense of personal and social responsibility—are reflected in the activities of the workplace. We spend a large part of our day at work. Nowhere does a greater opportunity exist for practicing ethical conduct than in this setting.

Yet, few companies require that their managers describe the ethical cost/benefit of a particular action in planning a marketing strategy or setting up annual budgets. Candidates for employment are seldom asked to describe how they have handled ethical dilemmas. When managers must make tough decisions about people or resources, all too rarely are plans for action described in terms of the company's ethical obligations. Rarely are salespersons who put integrity above making commissions visibly and formally recognized by their companies.

This book is designed to make ethics an on-the-table topic, and to make ethical actions part of the usual and customary way that business is done. It provides a framework that allows for the clear identification and implementation of strategies to improve the ethical climate in the workplace. This book also serves as a concise, practical text for students in business, organizational psychology, and ethics courses.

In the view of many business leaders, ethical commitments are personal. Someone either has them or does not have them. Ethical behavior is not viewed as a skill to be learned.

This book is dedicated to the view that ethical change is possible. Our goal is not just to talk about ethics but to help bring about ethical change. One of us (Clark) has a Ph.D. in philosophy and is a university professor of ethics, while the other of us (Lattal) has a Ph.D. in clinical psychology and is a management consultant for corporations. We have combined our areas of expertise to produce a book that is both philosophical and practical. Ethical behavior requires effective ethical thinking, but equally important, it results from practical strategies for saying and doing the right things in offices, factories, salesrooms, and everywhere business is conducted.

In the 1990s more than ever before, American business people have become aware of the essential role that an ethical outlook plays in the success of their companies. In part, this is because the field of business ethics—as both an academic discipline and a social movement—has expanded significantly in recent years. In part, it is because American businesses are transforming themselves in response to competitive pressures from Japan and other foreign countries. As the world acquires a global economy, profound changes are taking place in the field of business management. These changes have important implications for workplace ethics, both in the United States and around the world. The marketplace is becoming more hospitable to ethics.

Unquestionably, there exists a close connection between ethical behavior and profit. On the one hand, ethical companies avoid the negative consequences of unethical behavior, such as bad publicity, fines, and the legal expenses of defending themselves in court. On the other hand, they acquire all the benefits of a good reputation: loyal employees and business associates, easier recruitment of the most talented people, a stronger spirit of teamwork across all employee levels, higher morale, both new and old customers who are attracted to what the company stands for, suppliers who are more accommodating and reliable, goodwill from communities in which the companies operate.

Corporations are finding that being more ethical is a competitive advantage in the global economy of the 1990s. The "quality imperative" is redefining the terms of competition.

At the same time, someone who behaves more ethically simply to increase profits has failed to grasp what morality is all about.

Ethical values are the highest of all values, which means that being moral for the sake of profit undermines the very idea of morality. Moral values cannot exist in the service of other values. Instead, ethical actions have payoffs that transcend business, while providing a cornerstone upon which to build and run a business.

As far as the profit motive is concerned, the most that can be said is that being moral *usually* is the most profitable course of action. However, there is no guarantee that it will be.

Some people believe that the American business system itself must be overhauled in a radical fashion before significant moral improvement can occur in the workplace. We do not share that outlook. Radical change is not needed in the structure of society or in the ways we conduct business; rather, we need a great many small changes, all of which can add up to a workplace moral revolution. For such a revolution to take place, we need to bring ethics into the mainstream of debate and action in corporate board rooms, managers' forums, and the daily practices of employees. The commitment to ethics needs to be visible both inside and outside the corporation.

Critics sometimes say, "You cannot teach ethics." Our position is that clear expectations and consequences designed into the workplace can make a profound difference in people's behavior, including their ethical behavior. Moral leadership, discussion of ethical dilemmas arising from the day-in-day-out pressures and influences of the work environment, examples set by managers and co-workers, training sessions, statements of corporate values, and the corporate culture as a whole—all can make a most significant difference.

Apart from the effects of workplace expectations and consequences, some individuals strengthen their ethical commitments by means of personal experiences, education, reading and thinking, and the influence of friends. We do not believe that it is ever too late for a person to acquire new behavior and values.

Throughout this book, we make every effort to avoid a one-sided presentation of ideas and advice. For example, we acknowledge the role that religious beliefs can play in a person's moral outlook, but we do not rest our case on the viewpoint of any particular religion. We are aware of the contributions to ethical thought made by major theorists—utilitarian, Kantian, Aristotelian, etc. While we do not tie our orientation to any of these schools, it does contain insights from all of them.

Some academically oriented ethics texts say that ethical questions can be answered only when the single best fundamental moral principle has been arrived at and applied. A frequently discussed example of such a principle comes from utilitarianism: Everyone should strive to bring about the greatest good for the greatest number of people. Another example is Immanuel Kant's Categorical Imperative: Every genuinely moral action will generate its own universal moral law applicable to everyone. We have serious reservations about such "single moral principle" approaches to answering ethical questions in business, or anywhere else for that matter. Especially in difficult cases, no single basic moral principle is likely to be adequate. Instead, several different basic principles usually apply and in ways that conflict with one another.

Ethical decision-making involves evaluating the potential effects of decisions against the entire set of fundamental values. Because we see the real world as being much more complex and "messy" than the "single moral principle" approach allows, we are committed to a philosophy of *moral pluralism.*

For many people, it is all too easy to operate from the perspective of one or two cherished values, not measuring moral decisions against other competing and equally important values. From the perspective of moral pluralism, the best that anyone can do is act according to the general direction mapped out by one or another of the basic moral principles while achieving a compromise among competing values. In the chapters that follow, we will illustrate this approach through numerous examples.

Some people believe that being moral means following a set of rules. In reality, doing the right thing is much more difficult than following rules, regardless of what the rules are. We view prohibitions against lying, fraud, and stealing, to name only a few, as important in business ethics, but they are not fundamental. Much that goes wrong in the workplace does involve the violation of moral rules, but a deeper challenge lies in the formulation of principles and values that underlie rules. A still deeper challenge is finding effective strategies that integrate fundamental values more completely into human life as a whole.

A large majority of the business ethics books currently available are focused on ethical dilemmas at the highest levels of management. They concentrate on questions about the overall direction of business and society such as these: Should international corporations allow their representatives to bribe government officials in foreign countries where bribery is commonplace? Should the U.S. government strengthen or weaken affirmative action laws at home? In what ways should Congress improve insider trading legislation? Which environmental policies are best? Discussing such questions, whether in the classroom or elsewhere, is certainly worthwhile. However, major policy questions are not the ones faced on a day-to-day basis by most corporate managers, engineers, salespeople, secretaries, shop workers, advertisers, or accountants. For most people in the workplace, less momentous issues, such as how to treat customers, fellow workers, bosses, employees, or suppliers are the most important. "Small" matters often underlie the large ones.

In this book, we discuss ethical questions of all types—not just those faced by the highest levels of management. The advice we offer applies as much to entry-level positions in business as to high-level managerial positions.

Moral improvement, whether it be one's own or that of others, will not happen easily unless understanding is achieved in a number of different areas. In our teaching and consulting, we have come to think of attaining ethical enlightenment as being much like jumping over hurdles on an obstacle course. Some of these hurdles have to do with concepts and arguments in moral philosophy. Other hurdles involve an understanding of the ways that people interact with one another. To get to the end of the obstacle course, people in the workplace must know both *what to say* and *what to do*.

The first hurdle that we discuss in this book concerns misunderstandings in regard to moral integrity. On a personal level, each and every human being faces the need to achieve and maintain moral integrity. How one attains this is the subject of Chapter One. We describe what integrity means in the business world, why it is essential, and we present arguments and strategies for strengthening it.

The second hurdle is primarily a philosophical one. It is the need to overcome a widespread perception that business ought to play by its own rules. We address this issue in Chapter Two, which provides intellectual ammunition to be used against the "business is amoral" point of view. The same moral values that apply everywhere else are applicable in the world of business.

The next chapter, entitled "The Third Hurdle: Recognizing Individuality," focuses on the concept of being one's own person while respecting the autonomy of others. An ethical person respects the rights of others while still maintaining the capacity to make independent choices. We discuss examples of workplace conduct that undermine respect for individual autonomy, and techniques for eliminating such conduct.

In an important sense, all business consists of sales. We sell a product, a service, our talents, our ideas, and so on. We have devoted Chapter Four to the ethics of sales. It espouses the one message that above all others we want to convey to readers. Many of you doubtlessly believe the message already and follow it, but it is nevertheless worth repeating. *Success in business is a wonderful thing, but it can be achieved at too high a price.* Accordingly, the fourth and perhaps most difficult hurdle everyone faces in the workplace is learning how to achieve an appropriate balance of values in our business lives. Achieving such a balance is especially important in regard to sales, but the points we make in this chapter are sufficiently general that they apply to other aspects of business as well.

Chapter Five, "Making Ethical Decisions," has more to say about achieving an appropriate balance among conflicting values. Within the context of moral pluralism, we discuss basic ethical values: the moral concept of rights; helping those in need; the common good; and self-interest. This chapter provides a conceptual framework for making ethical decisions. It defines a decision-making model to use in evaluating ethical decisions at a personal or organizational level. A substantial part of the chapter is devoted to an analysis of examples.

In the next four chapters, we turn to the topics of personal and organizational change. In Chapter Six, "The Office Climate," we discuss ways to make office settings more conducive to ethical behavior. We use the expression "office settings" broadly to include all of the circumstances of work that make a job "more than a job." The advice offered in Chapter Six and in the following three chapters reflects current thinking about personal and organizational change. We describe steps to be taken to create workplaces that are both ethical and conducive to business success.

Chapter Seven addresses beliefs that may impede ethical change and processes that are fundamental to behavior change. Chapter Eight continues the discussion about change and the opportunity to establish conditions in the workplace that maintain ethical behavior. In both of these chapters, we describe workplaces where negative control of behavior through threats and punishments is replaced by incentives that encourage initiative, cooperation, and innovation. Managers are challenged to view themselves as being in a reciprocal relation with employees, influencing and being influenced by the changes each makes.

Chapter Nine, "Workplace Ethics and the Quality Imperative," builds bridges between contemporary management practices and a commitment to ethics. Chapter Ten explores workplace ethics in an international setting. Finally, Chapter Eleven contains implications for action in the workaday world.

# CHAPTER ONE

# The First Hurdle: Building Moral Integrity

The concept of moral integrity has a somewhat specialized meaning in the world of business: doing what is right regardless of expected profit. More precisely, moral integrity in business is the strength of character needed to do what is right regardless of expected financial gain or loss.

Although it may seem paradoxical, demonstrating moral integrity in business practices—doing the right thing for its own sake, regardless of profit or loss—can increase the likelihood that a business will be profitable. A person who does the right thing regardless of expected profit is just the person who may make the most money in the long run. Others will judge this person as one who can be counted on; such trust is fundamental to business success. Of course, there can be no absolute guarantee that this will happen. *In order to win, you must be willing to lose.*

What is there to win? This question has a number of different answers. Those who commit themselves to actions based on moral integrity measure winning other than in strictly financial terms. A person who has moral integrity welcomes any profits that result from upholding his or her integrity, but has no serious regrets if profits do not result. The primary motivation all along has been to do the right thing for its own sake.

Why should a person do the right thing simply for its own sake? That is, why should we place a high value, or any value at all, on moral integrity?

As human beings, we are many different people—women or men, executives or shop workers, lawyers or laborers, engineers or

9

clerks, athletes or artists, musicians or mathematicians. We are humorous or talkative or self-assured. These dimensions of ourselves are not the most important dimensions of human life. Imagine that two people are introduced at a party. Perhaps one of them is a salesperson while the other is a professional singer; or one of them is a certified public accountant while the other is a high school English teacher; or one might be an actress while the other is an industrial chemist. Perhaps one is extremely outgoing, telling one joke after another, but the other is quiet and introverted. People such as these, momentarily paired off in the midst of life's commotion, might feel that they have little in common. In reality, they could be more alike than any others who are paired off at the party—if they share the same values and each has the same moral integrity as the other.

People do not usually talk much about the things that really matter to them, particularly when they have first been introduced. Consequently, it is easy for two people at a party to talk briefly about pleasantries and then move on, never discovering that each shares the same moral values. They never discover that each believes as much as the other in respecting people's rights, keeping one's word, and honoring contracts. They both subordinate their own interests to other values when appropriate; they act on principle when that is the right thing to do and generally do not take the easy way out. They do what is right for its own sake.

In the deepest and most important sense, what we are as human beings is a reflection of how we go about making ethical choices in our own lives—what we stand for. Do we have moral integrity? Can people count on us to do what is right? Do we always put our own interests first, or do we also look out for the interests of other people? Are we committed to moral principles of rights, helping those in need, and the good of society? Have we thought about these principles and our reasons for following them? Have we thought about what to do when basic moral principles appear to conflict?

The people we admire most are those who exhibit the highest degree of integrity in their own lives and who are committed to values that go beyond themselves. We admire them even when we disagree with them. We admire them because of the difference they make in the world. We suspect that their lives are more significant than the lives of people who have not reached out beyond themselves to the same degree.

Values that matter the most to us as individuals are of equal importance in the world of business.

## THE ETHICAL PERSPECTIVE

A person with moral integrity wants to do what is right; in order to carry out this intention, a person needs to have a moral, or ethical, perspective on life. In the most general terms, this means (1) concern for others and respect for oneself and (2) a desire to achieve an appropriate balance between the two. Ethical behavior requires that in one way or another the interests of *all* affected human beings be taken into consideration, including oneself.

The actions of people who violate fundamental rights of others in order to promote only themselves clearly fall outside the sphere of ethical behavior. We may not know what such people believe their own motivations to be, but we can evaluate the effects of their actions. Those who kill others with no apparent compunction, sell drugs to children, or commit violent crimes for pleasure are undeniably acting outside the sphere of ethical behavior. Fortunately for the rest of us, such people are not encountered frequently in the workplace.

We are more likely to encounter individuals who *appear* to be concerned for others when in fact they care only for themselves. Their actions may frequently benefit both themselves and others. However, when they perceive other people as jeopardizing a personal objective, such individuals do whatever is in their own interest, regardless of who else may be harmed. When such manipulative but successful individuals are encountered in the workplace, they may be lauded for knowing what they want and going after it. When they violate individual rights, they may be called "gutsy" and "determined."

When we fail to identify their behavior as contrary to the company code, we foster the belief that such behavior is actually what is wanted—i.e., such actions are required to achieve profits. If we take the morally correct road or speak out for the good of others, we may be perceived as weak, naive, or unsophisticated. We might not measure up well against those "aggressive SOBs."

At the other end of the spectrum are people who never speak out for their own interests or confront an issue that might benefit themselves and others. Such passivity in an individual frequently leaves fellow employees alone in taking risks, while it discounts that individual's unique value to the organization. There is little or no reciprocity, or giving back to the organization in terms of the person's best advice or judgment. Such people are unreliable in terms of candor and genuine support; their passivity places particular burdens on others to take care of them. There is even an element of selfishness in their behavior in that it excludes the needs or wants of others. Such people often lack skill in speaking assertively and lack confidence in what they have to say or do. In their preoccupation with their own needs, they are likely to misread how their behavior affects others, and they may end up harming others without intending to do so.

Concern for others and respect for oneself are requirements for the ethical perspective. As we see it, the most basic moral value is what philosophers call the "intrinsic worth" of every human life: the value that all human lives have, *in and of themselves*. Disregarding the interests of others is wrong. It means that we do not recognize that the lives of these other people are valuable in and for themselves. At the same time, respecting the life that is our own supports the belief that all human life has value in itself. We recognize who we are and how our interests must be balanced with the interests of others. It is essential that we weigh these interests when evaluating the ethical aspects of our decisions. Ethical behavior requires balance.

## WHY BE MORAL?

What if doubts exist, not just about the application of moral[1] principles to business, but about the foundations of morality? In spite of good intentions, we may acquiesce in the face of unethical behavior and end up doing more harm than good. A weak response will only reinforce the idea that morality rests on a shaky foundation. Regrettably, moral beliefs can easily appear tenuous. The moral perspective may appear to conflict with pragmatic goals. People with the best intentions can fall prey to doubts and uncertainties. Weak responses by such people undermine moral integrity and make it impossible for them to be moral guides for others.

By contrast, it is easy to have the strong convictions of a skeptic! Why should I look out for the interests of customers, except when doing so is profitable? Why should I pay attention to my coworkers, when it won't pay me to do so? Or my employer? Or my employees? The people in my community? Future generations? Says the skeptic: There is no moral knowledge or genuine moral assurance. The above questions are too difficult. People have talked about morality for centuries, but no one has figured it out—no one has provided definitive answers. However, there is nothing mysterious about my wants and desires. I know that I need food, clothes, a house, and I would surely like to have an expensive car, luxurious vacations, and a summer home on the lake. Why should I sacrifice unambiguous values (my needs and wants) for ambiguous ones?

The advocate of morality in the workplace must go one-on-one against the forcefulness and clarity of the skeptic's point of view. The challenge is formidable. It can be summarized with a question:

## Why be moral?

This is the deepest and most difficult question in moral philosophy, but it is more than an academic question. At some point in life every reflective person is troubled by it. The person who finds no satisfactory answer to it may have no reason to apply moral standards in *any* sphere of life, not just the workplace. Such a person may act morally but without deep conviction, and thus may more easily try to justify and engage in unethical behavior. Such a person may lack an interest in making efforts to influence others in the workplace toward taking morality more seriously.

Moral integrity requires that we strengthen our moral convictions so that we can better challenge ourselves, as well as stand up to moral cynics. Are there answers to the question: Why be moral?

Let us start with an "easy" answer.

## The "Divine Command" Argument

This argument says that we should be moral because God wants us to be moral. God wills it. God wants us to care about all of our fellow human beings—to love others and recognize that "everyone is precious in God's eyes." While this may well be the best answer, its practical use is limited. Not everyone believes in God, and proof of God's existence has been notoriously difficult to achieve. Moreover, religious doctrines can exist in the name of God that place limits on who is to count as "precious," restricting the chosen circle to those who profess certain beliefs or share in a particular faith. Others are branded as unfit to enter God's kingdom.

Philosophers going back at least to the time of Thomas Aquinas in the thirteenth century have said that the ideal basis for morality is a combination of religious belief and rational argument. Let us turn to answers that do not depend solely upon religious belief.

## The Personal Satisfactions Argument

Apart from the religious explanation, one of the best reasons for being moral is what we call the Personal Satisfactions Argument. In essence, it says that people who choose to live moral lives will find their lives more satisfying than they otherwise would have been. People who choose to be moral in all spheres of their lives, both in their business activities and elsewhere, will be glad that they made this choice.

There is a catch, though. The satisfaction will likely be felt only some time *after* the choice to live a moral life has been made. People who already have a deep concern for their fellow human beings will be the ones who understand that virtue is its own reward—but they are not the ones who need convincing. Are there methods to convince people *now* that they ought to become moral or more moral than they presently are?

Some philosophers claim that it is simply impossible to appeal to values that a person does not yet have:

> Asked the skeptical question, "But why shouldn't I do actions that will harm others?" we may not know what to say—but this is because the questioner has included in his question the very answer we would like to give: "Why shouldn't you do actions that will harm others? Because doing those actions will harm others." The egoist, no doubt, will not be happy with this. He will protest that *we* may accept this as a reason, but *he* does not. And here the argument stops.[2]

James Rachels, a prominent American moral philosopher, appears to be saying that people are locked inside themselves with no way to break outside the circle of values to which they are already committed. There is no point in telling someone who puts self-interest first or exclusively that his or her actions harm others. If we attempt to persuade the egoist that he or she ought to be concerned for others, we will fail. The egoist simply cannot conceive that the lives of others have intrinsic value. If Rachels is correct, then the Personal Satisfactions Argument will fail where it is needed most.

Is it true that we are locked inside the circle of values that we presently have? What if we say to the egoist that if she were to *acquire* more concern for others, and were then to reflect back upon the sort of person she had been, she would prefer being the sort of person she then would have become. Why isn't this "try it, you'll like it" approach acceptable? Rachels appears to assume that people's values are unchanging. We reject his assumption. We submit that significant changes can be made in how individuals behave and in their attitudes.

We come to hold our values because of our history of learning. We are taught values directly and indirectly; actions we take both create and reinforce beliefs regarding values. It is often the case that a person initially does not know exactly what his or her own values are. Knowledge can come from studied examination of what is and is not important; it can come also from examining the choices we make in given situations. If we wish to gain knowledge of ourselves in this most fundamental way, we will likely have to enlist the aid of others. They can observe our actions and from them help us extrapolate our values.

It is true that experience teaches us how to get the things we want. At the same time, it teaches us *what* we want and do not want. The Personal Satisfactions Argument says that living a life in which we reach out to others will teach us an important lesson in regard to what we *will want* from our lives henceforth.

Many of us make the assumption that we are who we are. Change is both too costly and ineffective when it comes to those fundamental components of our personality we call "values." This notion that values cannot be changed allows us too often to excuse the unethical behavior of others, not to mention equivocating on our own ethical dilemmas in real-life situations. Is it true that a more moral life, one that is less self-centered and more other-directed, will eventually turn out to be a more satisfactory life? We, the authors, believe so, and we are not alone in our belief. A singular piece of wisdom can be extracted from the world's poets and storytellers on the one hand, and the philosophers and scientists on the other: The most meaningful and satisfying life is achieved by reaching out beyond the self. People who think primarily about themselves—their aches and pains, their accomplishments, their wants and needs and how they will fulfill them—live impoverished lives. Those who think primarily about business concerns that will benefit them in a narrow sense are poorer for it, and those around them in the workplace are also less well off. Paradoxically, the more someone pursues his or her own satisfactions in a dogged and single-minded fashion, the less satisfaction the person is likely to feel. The self that is tended so carefully will seem to slip away. Self-discovery often lies in actions that take one beyond the self.

For those readers who know how hard it is actually to change your own or someone else's behavior, we have included a discussion of behavioral change in Chapters Seven and Eight. Guidelines are provided for the establishment of new patterns of behavior. We discuss implications of the finding in psychology that if someone's behavior is changed for a period of time and the person is rewarded for the change, then the person's beliefs will likely change as well to support the new ways of acting. Change involves more than a desire to change. It requires setting up conditions to evoke and maintain the new behavior. Such behavior patterns, consistently applied over time, become who we are.

Because our sense of ourselves is shaped by what we do, "going along with the crowd" is more harmful than is often realized. It increases the likelihood that behavior we do not endorse will occur more frequently than if we had not acquiesced. In addition, much harm can result to oneself and others when individuals fail to speak up for fear of offending someone. When people play fast and loose with valued principles, their "conscience" or learned ethics may intercede at first, causing a feeling of guilt. Unfortunately, with practice, such guilt lessens considerably.

Compromising ethics leads to a compromised sense of ethics. Practicing moral actions leads to consistency of such action. Putting ourselves in situations where moral integrity is expected increases the likelihood that we will behave ethically. Companies that demand less than our best in terms of ethical commitment reduce the likelihood that we will act ethically when it is important to do so. We all have more powerful effects on one another than we may acknowledge or even know. Thus, it is incumbent upon all of us to support and protect the best aspirations of ourselves and others—as individuals, as a department, an office, a company, or as part of society at large.

## The Pragmatic Argument

In these closing years of the twentieth century, despite arms reductions and the ending of the Cold War, civilization is threatened by the sheer fact that nuclear weapons exist—tens of thousands of them stockpiled by the United States, the former Soviet republics, and other countries. Equally, civilization is threatened because technology has advanced so far that other horrendous uses of it have been and are being developed. Eventually these other uses of technology (chemical, biological, who knows what else?) may far surpass nuclear weapons in destructive power.

At the heart of many serious problems facing contemporary civilization is the apocalyptic force of technology itself—a force that could be unleashed in an instant during wartime, or unleashed more slowly in times of peace through pollution of the environment and the upsetting of natural balances that have been in existence for millions of years.

The Pragmatic Argument asserts that contemporary civilization will require great wisdom to overcome the dangers that it faces. A most important aspect of wisdom is morality, especially the idea that all human beings have intrinsic worth and therefore deserve concern and consideration. All of us must do whatever we can to strengthen both our own morality and that of others, both within the workplace and outside of it.

Technology is just beginning to demonstrate its incalculable benefits to humankind—in raised standards of living, medicine, communications, and global understanding. These benefits are too precious to lose as the consequence of myopic perspectives that lead to self-destruction. It is clear that the human race has much to gain in promoting the intrinsic worth of all individuals in the workplace and everywhere else.

## NOTES

1.  We use the terms "moral" and "ethical" and their variations interchangeably throughout this book.

2.  James Rachels, "Egoism and Moral Skepticism," in *Vice and Virtue in Everyday Life*, ed. Christina Hoff Sommers (New York: Harcourt Brace Jovanovich, 1985), p. 108.

# CHAPTER TWO

# The Second Hurdle: "Business Is Amoral"

This book joins a growing number of publications that address ethical issues in the business world. Not only has the number of books devoted to business ethics increased dramatically during the last ten to fifteen years, so has the number of journals and newsletters. Many more business schools now require ethics courses, numerous seminars and conferences concerned with moral questions in business are held around the country, and increasing numbers of corporations write their own codes of conduct and strengthen efforts to enforce compliance with these codes. The workplace is a significant component of our lives. It frequently mirrors changes that are currently occurring in our society, where more people are actively seeking ways to improve the quality of their lives. There is more talk about finding personal meaning in the workplace as well.

Yet even now large numbers of people remain virtually untouched by, and uninterested in, the "business ethics revolution" that is sweeping the country. They may believe that integrity is something for which one should strive in one's personal life, but that business decisions lie outside an ethical framework. Such people believe that business is not exactly immoral or unethical, but instead that "the business of business is business." We encounter these individuals in the workplace all too frequently—their attitudes strongly affect how they treat subordinates, co-workers, supervisors, customers, and the general public.

## THE AMORAL PERSPECTIVE

Business people cannot afford to evaluate business decisions according to ethical criteria. They must play the game—eat or be eaten, get the job done or face bankruptcy. Talk about "integrity," "acting on principle," "moral sensitivity," "conscience," and the like, is just so much window dressing. It covers up the reality that the business world follows its own rules, and these practices mean just one thing—SURVIVAL.

This is the idea that business is not so much immoral as *amoral*. It is exempt from some or all of the rules of morality, in contrast to other areas of conduct. People who express this point of view range from the blatantly dishonest to those who exhibit scrupulous honesty in all matters. All have in common the belief that making money is either the sole purpose of business or it is by far the most important.

Consider the following case, which is admittedly a stereotypical example of ethics in the hands of a used car dealer:

Frank owns a small auto repair shop. On the side, he sells cars that he has fixed. Frequently he buys them from customers whom he persuaded to sell "before repairs really get expensive." Even though it would not be true, he might say to a customer, "The engines in that model usually don't go much beyond 80,000 miles; you've been lucky."

Some of the cars that Frank sells need only cosmetic changes to be resold. He sets odometers back or replaces them with odometers from wrecked vehicles showing lower mileage. He tells customers that transmissions are in excellent shape even when they are faulty. He tells fictitious stories about each car's "pristine" history.

Frank talks about his business practices with like-minded friends, who see nothing wrong. "Anyone who wants to before they buy a car can take it to an independent mechanic to be checked out, but most people are too stingy for that. They want me to fix the cars before I sell them, keep them on my lot where they can get damaged and dirty, and are getting older every minute, costing me money. If my customers want cars that don't need any repairs, then they're better off buying new ones. People who buy used cars shouldn't complain if the transmission goes bad right away—what did they expect, buying a used car? If I

told them everything that was wrong, I would never sell anything. Besides, all the other dealers are telling the same stories
I am."

Would Frank do anything whatever to make a profit? No, of
course he would not. He would never embezzle money or rob a bank.
He would not dream of committing murder for profit. Moreover, he
would not be any more inclined to lie to his friends or associates
than the average person would be, although Frank does play fast and
loose with the truth when it comes to his auto business. He believes
business to be special, to have its own rules, and honesty is not one
of them. He convinces himself that people have unreasonable expectations and that his customers are not really bad off in the end.
He convinces himself that other dealers follow these same practices.
His own business practices fall at the low end of the honesty/dishon-
esty continuum.

Here is another case in point:

Mike is a wholesale distributor for produce. At harvest times
and other occasions when fruits and vegetables are plentiful,
Mike's business requires a large work force. However, during
winter, or when the harvest is bad, or consumer demand slumps
for one reason or another, Mike must reduce the work force.
He gives minimal warning before laying people off for weeks
or months, sometimes permanently. Occasionally employees show
up for work in the morning and he tells them they have been
laid off beginning that day—he never informs them for how
long. Most of his employees are people with few skills who
cannot get more secure jobs elsewhere.

"I promise them nothing beyond a day's fair wages for a
day's work because the market for produce is volatile. My job
as I see it is to deliver the best food for the lowest price—
period! I'm proud of the fact that I have been doing that for
twenty years. I'm still in business, unlike some of my competitors. The grocery chains that sell produce most economically
can depend on me to have the best stuff at the best prices, and
my employees can depend on me to offer them work if I have
it. That would not be the case if I went out of business. Sometimes they come to me begging for work after a layoff because
someone is sick or the mortgage is due or whatever, but that is
not my responsibility.

"They complain because I give no warnings before layoffs, but if I told them beforehand, they might quit early to look for work elsewhere. Anyway, I usually don't know myself how many people to lay off until the day arrives because market conditions are constantly changing. If I *promise* someone work for a certain period of time—which I do for the more skilled people whom I can't afford to lose—then I keep my promise. Likewise, if I say that a shipment of lettuce is fresh, then it is fresh. I tell an absolutely straight story to everyone."

Both Frank and Mike put the profitability of their businesses first, but Frank is largely unconcerned about the well-being of customers *and* dishonest while Mike appears dispassionate but honest in terms of being truthful to the people he employs and those with whom he has business dealings. He does express concern for the hardships faced by his employees when he lays them off, but he believes that business should not involve itself in such matters. He believes that he is doing a lot of good for society *just because* he puts making a profit ahead of everything else and because he is essentially honest as he sees it.

Mike might justify his actions using concepts similar to those Adam Smith employed in *The Wealth of Nations* (1776) to explain how, as Smith saw it, the private pursuit of self-interest through profit-making in business benefits the country as a whole under conditions of economic freedom. An "invisible hand," said Smith, will direct such activity toward the prosperity of society. Mike might go so far as to say that individuals like himself are the world's most moral people because they are the ones who get the job done. They are the ones who deliver the food, complete construction jobs on time, keep the country's lights burning and its wheels turning. In making money for themselves, they benefit the entire country. If morality means actually doing good, then they are moral because their businesses do a lot of good. Therefore, Mike might ask, what could be wrong with the way that he runs his business? Call it amoral if you will, he might say, but it's the best way to run a business.

## MORAL PURPOSES

We disagree with Mike's point of view. From our perspective, the best way to run a business is to run it as ethically as possible and that means considering matters other than the pursuit of profit. As we see it, being ethical means having a moral purpose in life—a purpose broader than making profits in an honest business.

A critic will ask: Does this mean that one ought to *sacrifice* profits for the sake of morality? If so, then aren't we forgetting about competition? In a competitive economy, every business must do whatever it can to make a profit or it will fall behind other businesses. Only the winners or near winners stay in the race. This has always been true, but in the global economy of the 1990s it is truer than ever before because foreign competition has intensified pressure on everyone. In a highly competitive economy, Mike's point of view may appear to be the only realistic one.

After all, critics will say, every dollar spent on workers who are less productive is charity; every dollar spent on the environment (unless government requires competing businesses to spend as much) is charity; every dollar not extracted from potential customers is charity; every dollar spent on the community that does not result in additional profits is charity. Every effort to give special consideration—beyond what will increase profits—to people with handicaps, minority groups, women, or the elderly is essentially charity.

A company that chooses to engage in charity will soon be out of business; every worker who does not do all he or she can to keep a job or prepare to find another will be at a competitive disadvantage. Businesses and everyone in them must do everything they can to survive. Even then, many will not survive. Companies will go bankrupt. Individuals will lose their jobs and not find replacements. If they do find other jobs, they will take a cut in salary or benefits. The margin for error is practically zero.

So the story goes. The world of business is truly amoral.

For proponents of this point of view, we have a number of questions, beginning with one addressed to Mike, the produce wholesaler. We want to know: Why, if making money is his single aim in business, does he "tell a straight story to everyone"?

He might say that doing so is the secret of his success. People trust him; in the food business, trust is especially important.

Unquestionably, trust is important in business. We believe that people frequently underestimate the extent to which scrupulous honesty enhances profit, especially over the long run. This is especially true now, when the quality imperative is revolutionizing business management. (We will have more to say about the quality imperative, or the quality movement, in later chapters.) Mike has been in business for twenty years and anticipates being in business another twenty. His reputation is his most valuable asset.

We have a second question for Mike: Would he continue to be scrupulously honest if his business were failing and his efforts of twenty years were going down the drain? Food wholesaling is a fiercely competitive segment of the business world; hard work and a good reputation do not guarantee continued success.

Suppose Mike answers in the negative: In a crunch, he says, he might be willing to abandon his policy of strict honesty. If this is his answer, then being honest may be the secret of his success in the good times, but it has a caveat attached to it. A person who is honest *only as long as it is profitable* may find that the need for immediate gain overrides honesty, especially in situations where competition is fierce. Therefore it is unlikely that "honesty" actually is the secret of Mike's success. More likely, his secret is opportunism and the effectiveness of using "honesty" as long as things are going well.

Let us suppose instead that Mike truly is scrupulously honest— that his answer to our second question is not negative but affirmative. He would be honest at all times, even if he found himself in bankruptcy court. If his business were hit hard by competitors with innovative methods that he wasn't able to adopt in time, he still would remain scrupulously honest rather than cut corners.

Why would Mike remain honest even when his business was failing? That is our third question. Why remain honest when he might be able to salvage something if he were willing to fudge on the truth?

Ideally, Mike will say that he tells the truth because it is simply the right thing to do. That is the kind of honesty that can be most counted on—the individual who is honest has learned that such integrity offers the greatest benefit. It is the right thing to do whether or not it can be measured in precise terms. Bona fide honesty, like other aspects of morality, exists for its own sake.

Therefore, if Mike really means it when he says that he is an honest man, he can answer our third question by saying that his life stands for something other than merely making money or pursuing his own interests. He stands for honesty first and making money second. The first goal will not be sacrificed for the second.

This leads us to our fourth and last question for Mike: If he places honesty above profit-making in his scheme of values, why isn't he willing to place *other* values as well above profit-making? We mean values such as kindness toward his employees and regard for the well-being of people in his community. Perhaps because of competitive pressures, he cannot do much more than he is now. However, at the very least, the well-being of his employees should count equally with his concern for honesty. Furthermore, if he has been able to save a substantial portion of his profits over the years, then he may even be in a position to earmark some part of these savings to help his employees when he lays them off.

Presumably, those who defend the claim that business is amoral and who admire the way that Mike runs his firm would have us believe that honesty is somehow in a class by itself: It is merely a decision-point to consider in "playing the game" of business, not a higher value. It is part of the pursuit of profit, at least for some businesses such as Mike's. It is relatively easy for Mike to tell a straight story about his merchandise because he deals with a product that everyone agrees is valuable. People do not need persuasion to eat fresh fruits and vegetables. The situation is different for a business selling a dubious product such as a wrinkle-reducing face cream that is not effective. Telling a "straight story" in such a case is not likely to be perceived as one of the essentials in the game of business by those who believe that profit-making comes first.

## THE DILEMMA OF BUSINESS ETHICS

Defenders of the amoral view of business tend to paint a black and white picture: Either a company does all it can to make profits or it totally abandons the pursuit of profit in order to engage in something other than business—we will label it charity.

The choice we have is not that stark, though. In other areas of life no one lives by a single value—why should business be an exception?

Devoted parents put a lot of effort into raising their children, but find time for other pursuits as well. If they do not, they seriously jeopardize the care they provide their children. Dedicated performers—musicians, actors, athletes—put a lot of effort into their careers as people must in any competitive field. But the person who subordinates everything to his or her career appears at best single-minded—at worst a fanatic. If the person goes so far as totally to neglect duties to children, then clearly the reach for success has gone too far. It is no longer simply an autonomous search for perfection but is, in fact, an abusive disregard for others. Needless to say, harm to oneself can occur as well.

Success can be achieved at too great a price—virtually every-one knows that. Why should the world of business be an exception?

The "dilemma of business ethics" can be put this way: If a business is moral, it will lose out to competitors; if it fights for survival, it will be driven to give up morality. Perhaps the key to resolving this dilemma lies in the value of products and services that a company produces and the commitment of the company to its employees and investors and the general public—its stakeholders. After all, business and ethics are intertwined. From the first moment a company decides to sell a tangible product or provide a service, its approach to these activities begins to establish an ethical framework.

## FACTORY CLOSINGS

Consider the situation of a corporation that must close a plant for sound economic reasons:

> Sharon is manager of a factory located in a small community where its closing will affect not only the employees of the plant and their families, but also people who run support businesses such as stores and gas stations, employees of local schools and government, and those who depend upon revenue to the local economy and tax base provided by the company. The harm caused to the lives of all these people, if the factory closes, will be direct and in many cases severe.
>
> Moreover, if the plant is closed, the company itself will be harmed. For example, anger expressed by displaced employees may jeopardize the company's public image as well as lower the morale of its remaining employees. But foreign competition and a downturn in the economy have made the plant unprofitable. What should be done?

First, before the company takes any official action, Sharon needs to carefully assess the special ethical considerations she faces as the plant manager, the one who will implement company decisions. She needs to evaluate the issues of power and how decisions about such massive events as plant closings will affect others. Regardless of what the company may do, Sharon has her own responsibilities. These responsibilities are all the more significant because she, in acting for the company, is expected to achieve the closing as smoothly as possible. She would do well to consider her own personal ethical obligations as a first step in addressing the question of what should be done.

It may well appear that the leaders of the company are insensitive to the consequences that their exercise of power has on others. Such appearances are not unique to people in business. It is just as easy for business managers to abuse their positions of authority as it is for people in government, the military, or police—or for a husband over a wife or a teacher over a student. In implementing change, those with power have a special responsibility to handle themselves carefully and to approach the change with as much visible respect for the well-being of others as is possible. This is particularly essential in situations such as the closing of a factory, or actions that in other ways risk the livelihood of individuals.

Perhaps the most important word is "visible." It does matter what and how things are said. It does matter that leaders speak forthrightly to employees. It does matter whether or not they have a plan that evaluates the "people costs" and that they do what they can to address those costs. Even when the closing of the plant must occur regardless of the harm to individuals, it is important that a review be conducted and its conclusions be seriously considered when anticipating the change. While others may misunderstand the motives and concern of the company, it remains incumbent upon those who have fiduciary responsibility to do what they can to minimize damage. It is wrong for them simply to make a decision and walk away.

Defenders of the amoral view of business say that in the tough competitive markets of today, businesses cannot afford to engage in charity that will lead them to bankruptcy. It does not matter whether the beneficiaries are employees, communities, the environment, or future generations. Our position is that businesses *can* afford to be moral and that such acts will not put them in jeopardy of bankruptcy. We advocate that a company combine the pursuit of profit with moral values in every situation where such values are relevant. This engagement in moral actions—giving back to others, concern for the well-being and greater good of employees, and actions geared to support the long-term health of the company—should be evaluated against pragmatic concerns.

A company will not be around long enough to act morally if it gives back so much of its margin to employees that it has little capital left to upgrade equipment, invest in new facilities, or take innovative risks. A company that does good through what it produces might be said to have a moral obligation to manage itself wisely. It looks toward the long-term health and well-being of its stakeholders (as well as its stockholders)—the community, consumers, employees and their families, and its investors.

What about companies that sell questionable products, use misleading advertisements, or engage in other objectionable business practices? There is no good reason why such businesses ought to survive in a tough competitive battle with other companies whose products and practices are superior. As an example, the world would unquestionably be better off without Frank's used car business.

Some companies produce a combination of worthless and valuable products. What about them? If their success is still possible without the worthless products, then they ought to drop them. If they cannot make a profit without products or services that have no value, then from an ethical perspective, their existence cannot be justified, even though they may be quite successful in the marketplace.

## DEGREES OF ASSISTANCE

How much help should a corporation give to those who are harmed by the shutdown of a factory or other crisis? No precise answer is possible, just as no precise answer is possible to the similar question of how much each of us as individuals ought to give to charitable causes. Many factors are relevant in making a decision. A necessary question to ask ourselves when deciding how much we as individuals should give to charity is simple enough: How much money do we have available for this purpose? In turn, an executive who faces a plant closing must ask: What cash reserves does the corporation have? What are its credit lines at the present time? Second, as individuals we should ask: What personal obligations do we have to families and friends and others that may conflict with giving a significant part of our income to charity? Similarly, an executive must ask: What needs does the corporation have to reinvest in new equipment at its other sites to keep them from closing? What is the extent of corporate debt? Third, as individuals it is appropriate for us to ask: What have we given already to other charities? What have we done to help others? An executive might ask: How much good has the corporation already done to help its employees and others? A corporation that has a good track record in this regard must still evaluate its situation in light of new needs or hardships that the closing creates. It should at least have in place procedures and programs that benefit employees now facing termination—such as a strong retirement system, a training and development program that keeps employee skills up-to-date, contingency funds to see people through a period of transition, and effective coordination with union officials to ensure that trust and communication are built into the fabric of the operation. Furthermore, unfavorable developments should be managed *before* the major crisis of a closing. This would greatly facilitate damage control. Companies that have never faced up to such obligations will have a more difficult challenge in managing the closing of a factory in an ethical manner.

## ABUSES OF LEGITIMATE POWER

Executives of large corporations need to constantly remind themselves that they can abuse their power, even if, as is usually the case, they acquired it legitimately. Power acquired legitimately is likely to produce complacency both in those who wield it and in those whom it affects. Most executives have risen to positions of authority as the result of talent and hard work, and it is appropriate for them to feel a sense of accomplishment. However, this feeling may blind them to their moral responsibilities.

In addition, executives are often cut off from a full evaluation of their effectiveness. Quarterly profits and losses provide them with significant feedback and such information is an appropriate and tough measure of accountability. However, many executives can go through their entire careers being measured only by this yardstick, no matter what else they may or may not do. Measurements by other yardsticks, such as how well they have treated employees or the quality of service they have provided to customers, may actually increase profit. The executive may further find that differential measurements across the spectrum of his or her activities provide personal, as well as professional, benefits.

Executives often do not receive the kind of candor they need from those closest to them. They absolutely must arrange their workplace environments to ensure that they will hear from those who will speak candidly. Executives need to deliberate with those with whom they disagree, being open to new ways of looking at traditional activities, and always examine their actions in terms of ethical implications. Some of these activities are typically viewed as outside the usual lines of accountability. Those who tell executives only what they seem to want to hear do not serve them well.

Seeking moments of reflection should not be optional, but rather a part of the fabric of a chief executive's life on the job. This is especially true during very difficult times of transition such as factory closings, mergers, and acquisitions. Without structured support for putting reflection ahead of other activities, most people, including executives, will get caught up by rapidly approaching events. The best time to consider actions that have ethical implications is before the storm. If senior executives accept this in-depth accountability, they are more likely to create a broader workplace affinity for dealing with issues such as the common good, fairness, and integrity.

## THE INTERESTS OF STOCKHOLDERS

Sometimes people say that corporate executives have an obligation to their stockholders to make as much money as possible. If stockholders want to give to charity, they could do so directly, rather than invest in the company. However, consideration of the role that stockholders play in business does not change what we have been saying. We need only ask: Would the stockholders, in their own lives, choose to put all their efforts toward single-minded endeavors regardless of the costs to others? Most would not. Then why would they want their financial investments to be any different?

What appears to happen is that we allow a depersonalized sense of ownership to work its way into stockholders' perceptions when we do not inform them of all the costs and benefits. If stockholders were informed about moral struggles such as those involved in a plant closing, many would be willing to invest in companies that combine the pursuit of profit with a firm commitment to moral values.

It is time for business leaders to start talking about the ethical nature of how and why their companies do business. Stockholders, employees, and consumers must have a stake in maintaining such a vision. It is important for business people at all levels of authority to vigorously challenge the amoral view of business.

# CHAPTER THREE

# The Third Hurdle: Recognizing Individuality

In this chapter, we discuss some of the conditions that promote respect for individuality.

## FOLLOWING MORAL RULES

Joe, who is an office manager, assigns an easier work schedule to his friend Henry than he does to Stan, with whom he doesn't get along. Both employees share the same job description.

Jennifer, a typist, continually finds excuses to leave her desk in order to check her makeup, get a drink, and stretch her legs. It seems to her office mates that she is seldom available when needed.

Jack, an accounts manager, takes home printer ribbons, mailing envelopes, rolls of tape, and other supplies. At home, he never buys these items. He has enough to give to his children and friends.

Lucy, who handles purchasing, often misses work for the slightest of reasons and frequently on days when the most work needs to be done.

Brenda, the company treasurer, is always late for work, for meetings, and even for luncheon engagements with clients and colleagues. The amount of other people's time that she wastes is considerable.

When you read about or encounter examples of workplace conduct such as these, what is your response? More than likely, you will ask yourself questions such as the following.

Why is Joe unable to see that he is abusing his position of

31

authority? He is increasing the friction between himself and Stan, and contributing to resentment between Stan and Henry. This interferes with effective office operations, shortchanging the company he works for. He is not playing the game according to long-established rules of fairness that are essential in a civilized society.

Why can't Jennifer see that she is violating her employment contract and thus is not playing by the rules? It makes no difference ethically whether the contract is written or oral, implicit or explicit. A person who takes a job agrees to work with a certain level of diligence, a level that Jennifer has fallen below.

Why can't Jack see that he is violating one of society's most basic rules, the prohibition against stealing?

We can submit similar questions to Lucy and Brenda.

All refer to the idea of *moral rules*. In earlier chapters, we said relatively little about moral rules. While they are extremely important for living in a civilized way, absolutely essential in fact, they are not fundamental. This point is frequently misunderstood. People make the mistake of supposing either that moral rules alone constitute morality (morality means following rules and nothing else) or that the essence of morality is "following your feelings" and rules do not count.

In fact, rules belong to the "surface" of morality; the essence of morality consists of deeper values, such as the intrinsic worth and dignity of all human beings (discussed below) and rights and justice (discussed in Chapter Five). If a person accepts those deeper values, then that person demonstrates respect for moral rules. This means that the person recognizes that a good reason is needed to justify breaking a moral rule.

Achieving ethical improvement in the workplace requires, among other needed changes, increasing respect for moral rules. One method is to bring such rules to the attention of people in the workplace. For example, publish and conspicuously post a company "Code of Conduct" that defines rules regarding company and individual property rights, the honoring of business and personal contracts, and the protection of personal and in some cases corporate privacy. We will say more about codes of conduct in later chapters.

However, it is not enough simply to focus attention on rules. As we just said, morality consists of much more than rules. In addition, it would be difficult in a manageably brief Code of Conduct to list all of the rules that should be taken into account. If a rule is not listed, does that mean it is unimportant? Needless to say, it does not.

Perhaps the most important first step that anyone can take to help bring about ethical improvement in the workplace or anywhere else is to "talk ethics"—exploring options, debating choices, defending ethical conduct, praising what is right, and condemning what is wrong. Ethical talk must be broadly focused, pushing people beyond the surface phenomena of moral rules. Rules help define appropriate actions, rules summarize those actions, but they are not alone sufficient to produce ethical behavior.

As children we were told: Wash your hands before meals. Never run into the street. Finish your homework before you go out to play. Come home before dark. Do not step in puddles. Make your bed before breakfast. Turn off the lights. Be quiet when others are sleeping. The rules of childhood were seemingly endless, and people carry their childhood with them in one form or another, along with an inclination to rebel against childhood. Moreover, it is not difficult for both children and adults to see that rules have exceptions. Sometimes playing is more important than homework. Sometimes there is a good reason not to make one's bed before breakfast. Sometimes it is okay to run across the street, step in puddles, or leave the lights on.

Because moral rules also have exceptions, effective "ethical talk" focuses on the reasons behind rules as much as on the rules themselves. It focuses on values. But here as elsewhere in discussions of ethics, nothing is simple and straightforward. It is not sufficient to check off a list of values one by one. In each instance of ethical choice there exists a hierarchy of values, some more important than others. However, from our perspective, there is a fundamental value that in all instances must be considered first.

## THE INTRINSIC WORTH OF ALL HUMAN BEINGS

As we see it, the most basic of all moral values is the intrinsic worth and dignity of all human beings. In the history of civilization, the highest kind of moral advancement has been the increasing recognition that in the most profound moral sense, all human lives count equally. Josiah Royce, an American philosopher of the late nineteenth and early twentieth centuries, called this the "moral insight."

Other people are selves just like us. They are valuable to themselves just as we are valuable to ourselves.

Most systems of morality in earlier times were "tribal" in recognizing the intrinsic worth of at least some of the members of one's own society (women and children did not always count) but not the intrinsic worth of people outside one's own society. Recent rights movements are current indications of our country's struggle toward moral progress. We are more concerned about such issues as civil rights, women's rights, and the rights of children, the elderly, homosexuals, and people with handicaps.

In the closing years of the twentieth century, most of us now acknowledge the inherent equality and worth of all human beings. Unfortunately, the human race has yet to act effectively on this recognition.

## INDIVIDUAL AUTONOMY

A recognition that people have intrinsic worth means several different things; the most fundamental is respect for autonomy. A rough definition of autonomy in this context is "being one's own person." An autonomous individual has opportunities to make his or her own choices, even wrong ones, within a broad range of actions. We must have rules regarding property rights, privacy, honoring contracts, truthfulness, etc., if autonomy is to be respected.

People have different interests, wants, and needs that can and do conflict. Life is full of hardships, deprivations, imperfections. For the majority of us, it is not exactly a vale of tears, but neither is it a cotton candy existence. From various religious perspectives (Judeo-Christian, Muslim, Hindu, and many others), life is a testing ground for everyone—a harsh testing ground for some.

In a world like ours, individual autonomy requires the existence of an "impersonal structure" to life that only rules can provide. The rules must not depend upon the whim, or even the considered judgment, of others. For each of us to "be our own person" day in and day out, we must be in a position to expect that most people will follow the rules.

Rules give us space to be ourselves: If it is *my* property, then (within established limits) I can do what *I* want with it. Because one's sexuality belongs within one's own private sphere of life, a person can make of it what he or she wants. Invasion of another's privacy is intolerable. Unless we keep promises and honor contracts, we will be unable to carry out plans that involve interactions with others. If we do keep our promises and honor agreements, then cooperation is possible—even with people who do not share our specific goals.

Because human beings too often fail to follow moral rules, a legal system is required to apply constraining influence where and when appropriate. The laws of the land, provided they are good laws, are an extension of moral rules and equally essential for the protection of individual autonomy. Thus, belief in the intrinsic worth of one's fellow human beings goes hand in hand with respect for rules and laws. The fundamental message is that we will treat others as we would have them treat us—as independent beings. Each possesses his or her own talents, achievements, hopes and aspirations, fears and uncertainties, and all of the burdens that humans endure, both self-imposed and those resulting from each person's unique station in life.

## WHEN GOOD PEOPLE BEHAVE UNETHICALLY

We all have a pretty good idea about what goes wrong when a "bad" person behaves unethically—the person lies, steals, reneges on contracts, ruthlessly takes advantage of others' weaknesses, and so on. This is blatant disregard for ethical norms. "Good" people also behave unethically, less blatantly but nevertheless in ways that can cause harm to other human beings as well as to themselves.

One of the most frequently occurring ways that "good" people behave unethically involves violations of individual autonomy. Examples: Well-meaning parents who choose careers or lifestyles for their offspring. Spouses who do not give each other enough room to develop as individuals. Conscientious people who attempt to push their political or religious beliefs onto friends or fellow workers. Employers who perceive female workers stereotypically as not being able to handle tough decisions.

It is all too easy for one person to fail to perceive the uniqueness of someone else. Even people who strive to be ethical can fail, as seen in the following examples.

A boss might have a rigid moral guidepost that requires him to treat everyone equally. He imposes an inflexible vacation schedule on his employees. One of his employees gets an invitation to visit

Paris for a week; even though she is not crucial to company activities for that week, the boss will not let her go.

A manager sometimes transfers subordinates in order to keep things running without any kind of disruption to production. This may require that employees move from the downtown location to one of the branch operations. There is no consideration of what the transfers may mean to personal lives and no attempt to work out problems. In some cases the transfer will mean increased costs for transportation and an extra hour of travel to and from work, increasing child-care time and time away from home.

A "company climate" that grows out of positive team spirit may compel employees to work longer than the normal workweek. The implied, but not necessarily proclaimed, rule is: "If you are really part of the team, you will put in a lot of time after normal hours. We notice those who go home right at five o'clock."

As far as the examples listed above are concerned, it probably does not occur to the decision-maker that he or she has unreasonable expectations. "I do it this way to achieve a greater good as I see it." It is important to bring to the attention of such people how an impersonal process such as unconditionally following rules can affect the autonomy of others.

The individual who refuses to help a colleague facing a deadline for the sole reason that "it is not right to do people's work for them" may be responding to rules learned early in life that at a rather simple level are correct. But when put in the context of cooperation, empathy, and respect for autonomy, such "absolutes" lose their moral strength and become hollow and empty.

Ethical behavior in the workplace is more than just "being true to one's own values." Just as much, it is a matter of having the right values in the first place. The highest level of ethical behavior requires an awareness of moral rules *and* the values they represent. We must weigh the relevant principles, gather all necessary information, and ask ourselves whether or not we are being morally sensitive to all the people we affect. We must decide when to follow rules strictly and when to make exceptions.

## CONSCIENCE

Many people believe that morality means "listening to one's conscience." Philosophers sometimes refer to the conscience as the "moral sense." They have debated at length about the role that it plays or should be allowed to play in ethical decision-making. Conscience from a behavioral perspective refers to our personal histories of reinforcement for conforming to certain societal standards.

We believe that listening to one's conscience is a skill that can be strengthened and put to good use, but we also believe that a person's moral feelings can and should sometimes be changed—at least "nudged" in a more favorable direction. A person's conscience is not an absolutely reliable guide for making ethical decisions.

If we are to respect the individuality of our fellow human beings, we must "listen to our conscience" in an enlightened way. The adult conscience often must reach beyond rules that do not apply exactly to the situations in which we find ourselves.

## AN ETHICAL FRAMEWORK

The application of the ideas we have discussed in this chapter provides a beginning point in developing public and measurable standards against which to evaluate ethical choices. Using these ideas to assess and validate our actions will constitute first steps toward being more fully accountable for ethical behavior at work. In the chapters that follow, we will spell out additional steps.

Unhappily, discussing the ethical criteria against which we measure our actions, whether those of our companies or those of ourselves as individuals, are steps we in the workplace all too rarely take. In this age of public accountability, it behooves both individuals and corporations to pay close attention to ethical decision-making and what it involves. We must go beyond simple declarations which proclaim that "the company always strives to do the right thing."

Too often both employers and employees do not know how to evaluate their actions against the elusive and difficult framework we call ethics. It can be done. When actions in the workplace are assessed against such a framework, the likelihood is increased that the commitment to, and benefit from, ethical behavior in the workplace will be seen as part of the corporate culture and fundamental to "how we do business."

# CHAPTER FOUR

# The Fourth Hurdle: Achieving Ethical Sales

Although nothing has greater importance to any business than selling its products or services, it is difficult to find a more ambiguous area of contemporary life. Without sales, a company loses its reason for existing. Yet many people are unsure what to think about the practice of selling. Should they aspire to it or despise it? Should they accept selling as a necessary evil, a marginal good, or a praise-worthy activity requiring a high level of skill?

Willy Loman in *Death of a Salesman*, who must make a living in a rough and tumble world where no quarter is given, elicits sympathy. The proverbial seller of used cars is distrusted, while "sales engineers" for large corporations are seen as belonging to a corporate elite who help to strengthen the American economy. A century ago it was the seller of horses who was distrusted, while employees of Great Britain's East India Company, engaged in foreign trade on a grand scale, were admired. Some people joke about the "traveling salesman." Many people look for ways to develop resistance to various sorts of sales pitches, while books such as *The Art of the Deal* become best-sellers. Especially within their own companies, successful salespeople may be heroes, but they are just as often mistrusted. Employees may advise one another not to be taken in by their "sophisticated" sales colleagues whose skills are equated with manipulative, self-serving strategies to achieve goals.

When it comes to sales practices, people are fascinated, envious, repulsed, grateful, embarrassed, and much else besides.

These attitudes should not be wholly unexpected because "selling" in a broad sense permeates life, and life is full of ambiguity, conflict, and controversy. Almost everything that people want in their lives requires convincing someone else to help provide it. It might be money, goods, services, friendship, security, or wider acceptance of a cherished belief. When we want something, we must convince others that they ought to give it to us, sell it to us, help us make it, or help us keep it. This means that we must make a case—we must sell our point of view. All sales involve a "sales presentation," even if this amounts to no more than placing ourselves in a position where we may hope that others will notice our needs and wants.

The heading for this chapter is perhaps misleading because the ethics of sales is not a separate branch of ethics with its own special rules. As we said in Chapter Two, the world of business is part and parcel of the world itself, not an "amoral" appendix. The arena of sales does not constitute a separate domain but rather is an important thread in the fabric of life. Nevertheless, a separate chapter is appropriate because some of the pressures that come to bear upon a career in sales are unique. Businesses have special obligations to examine how they design the financial incentives and goals of salespersons in order not to prompt or condone inappropriate actions. Also, we need especially to consider the ethics of sales just because selling is something we all do, regardless of our positions.

## WHAT GOES WRONG

Selling lies at the heart of all business activity. There is nothing "dehumanizing" about selling goods, services, one's labor, or anything else. (Except one's integrity! But doing that involves a different sense of the word "sell.") A career in sales will not necessarily make a person materialistic, greedy, grasping, or superficial. It need not teach a person "the price of everything and the value of nothing"—to quote Oscar Wilde. A career in sales can be as honorable as any other.

Unfortunately, pressures unique to sales can produce less than honorable actions. Far too often, sales activity is driven by short-term contingencies—bonuses, commissions, numbers on sales charts. Not making the sale, regardless of the reason, is almost never rewarded financially. Almost never is an "ethics credit" put in the salesperson's file for placing integrity above commission. In order to reassure the customer that what is said in the sales presentation is true, salespeople sometimes tell customers that a particular sale involves no commission. Even if such a statement is true, the need to say it indicates that something clearly is wrong.

A division frequently exists within a company between designated salespeople and other employees. The division may imply differences in status, training, and the degree of risk-taking expected. Yet, the common values *shared* by salespeople with their fellow employees are the most important in the long run and, in the vast majority of selling situations, are critical to success: courtesy, sympathy for others and especially for those in need, respect for the individuality of other people, and a desire to make some contribution toward improving the world. In other words, salespeople, like all other employees, are obligated to protect people's rights, alleviate suffering, and improve society overall—even in the tasks of routine business life. Salespeople must be concerned about the well-being of others while also looking out for their own interests in a responsible fashion. What is true of salespeople is true of everyone.

Consider the following example:

Jim Smith sells real estate. Not long ago, he sold a small house to a single parent, Sarah, who recently moved into town with her two children. She received no child support from her ex-husband and was struggling to make ends meet. She told Jim that she wanted to buy a house, in part, to build financial security—a correct observation several years earlier when the real state market was strong, but not as certain now. In Jim's town, real estate prices had peaked and were beginning to fall. As was his practice with every potential customer, Jim said nothing negative concerning the real estate market to Sarah; it was not his responsibility. If he were to tell potential customers that real estate is not a particularly good investment now, then fewer people would buy property. The market would get worse, setting up a self-fulfilling prophecy.

The house that Sarah showed the most interest in was one that had many small problems. Sarah was inexperienced in matters pertaining to building construction, furnaces, wiring, plumbing, etc. Jim said nothing about small problems that Sarah did not notice herself. The house was most suitable for owners who could make a lot of minor repairs themselves; it was a "fixer-upper," but Jim did not tell Sarah that.

Jim justified rushing Sarah into buying that particular house in part because he was not pushing her into offering the highest possible price for the property. The owner had the house listed for $72,000, but Jim knew he would accept an offer as low as $60,000. To make a quick sale, Jim told Sarah that the owner had turned down an offer of $58,000 but would probably accept $61,000. As Jim saw it, it was better for him to sell quickly two houses at the low end of their price range than to take a long time to sell one house at the high end.

The world is full of Jim Smiths—salespeople in every field who are not totally wrong in their moral thinking, but who fail to achieve a proper balance among values. They believe that customers should look out for themselves, which is true, but not to the degree that Jim required of Sarah. Jim required more of Sarah than was proper, considering her background and limited knowledge. Salespeople and their managers should establish a process that requires making more of an effort to understand their customers' situations than Jim made. Further, as a representative for the seller, Jim needed to keep the seller's interest more in mind and make a stronger effort to get the highest price for a property being sold. In Chapter Eight, we have more to say about the ways that salespeople and others can be helped to do a better job in these regards.

## FINDING AN APPROPRIATE BALANCE

Consider what Jim told Sarah about the real estate market. A positive attitude about the product on the part of salespeople is not morally wrong. Salespeople are essentially *advocates* for products or services; their job is to present what they are selling in an appealing light. What Jim did in persuading Sarah to buy the house went beyond that. He took advantage of someone who was struggling financially and who would probably have been better off not buying a house at the time that she did. Without question, she would have been better off not buying that particular house.

Sellers need not mention every last defect in a product or service, but should mention more of them than Jim did. From an ethical, as well as legal, point of view, they absolutely must mention all major defects; Jim was prepared to do this. They have an obligation to make a significant effort toward matching up the right product or service with the right customer. For Sarah, who had little money available for repairs and no skills of her own, all of the small problems with the house taken together amounted to a major problem. This issue was ignored by Jim in his eagerness to make a quick commission.

Salespeople have a stronger obligation to the people who hire them than was recognized by Jim. They should achieve a more appropriate three-way balance among the interests of the customer, the seller, and themselves. If Jim had been more candid with Sarah, then held out for a more suitable buyer for the house, he could have bargained more aggressively with that buyer. He would have produced both a more satisfied home owner in the long run and a more satisfied seller.

Why so many Jim Smiths? Is it because the United States—and much of the world—is so highly competitive that people are driven into behaving unethically? Is it that we espouse short-term goals and quick fixes? Is it that our society strongly endorses self-interest and individualism, and successful individuals are measured to a great extent by the money they make?

Certainly, societal emphasis on competition and winning, two highly acclaimed components of American business, might be interpreted loosely to justify selfish acts, but in our opinion they are not the true culprits. On the contrary, there is value in a free, or relatively free, market system where business is *open* to competition. Whether or not competitors will in actuality fight one another tooth and nail is another question. Within a market system that allows as much competition as possible, an appropriate balance of interests needs to be achieved by those who compete. A competitive marketplace does not preclude cooperation. In later chapters we discuss further the role that cooperation can play within a competitive marketplace.

Competition for sales does exert strong pressures on salespeople such as Jim Smith, but there is nothing unique about these pressures. They bear heavily upon people in other lines of work as well. There are pressures upon physicians to spend too little time with each patient, upon researchers to cut corners in collecting data, upon professors to grade students' papers in too much haste, upon farmers to use excessive amounts of pesticides, upon composers to appropriate musical ideas from others. The list is long.

In every walk of life there are conflicting values that must be balanced, particularly in cases where success requires measuring up to the achievements of other people or to monetary goals. There are temptations to spend too little time at one's job in order to have more time available for one's family. There are also temptations to spend too *much* time at one's job and too little with one's family. There are temptations to favor one's employers over one's subordinates, and there are temptations to do exactly the opposite. Everyone in the workplace faces pressures from many different and conflicting directions.

Some commentators say that the pressures in a sales career are unique because they are often one dimensional—all of the pressures are exerted in the direction of sales volume (measured in dollars or numbers of orders). In other areas of life there is a recognition that conflicting values do and should exist.

We expect people to seek a compromise between time spent with family and time spent on the job. The same applies to time spent on students and on one's research, or between loyalty to one's employer and one's subordinates, and so on. However, when a person is carrying out the proper functions of a salesperson, often one is expected to focus exclusively on volume and profits.

If the preceding were a correct characterization of sales practices, such practices would be amoral. It would be appropriate to liken the amorality of sales to the amorality of war; both have seemed to possess a single motivation, namely to win at all costs. "All is fair in love and war," people say.

Yet, the mark of a truly civilized world is the attempt to "civilize" warfare. We produce rules of war, as expressed in the Geneva Convention. These outlaw a considerable number of abhorrent practices, such as shooting prisoners and using chemical and biological weapons. Hence, not even war is one dimensional; even when one's life is at stake, not everything is permissible. If war can be civilized, then so can sales practices.

The point we wish to make is that sales *need not* be one dimensional. Indeed, a great many salespeople do have a keen sense that they are selling not only the product or service of their company, but also the commitment, promises, and follow-through they exercise as individuals. Salespeople, perhaps more than most other employees, represent themselves when representing the company. This perspective is not lost on the majority of people in sales departments, who sell with honesty and personal integrity. The longer term effect of what is said and done by salespeople builds a reputation; the protection of one's reputation provides a safety valve that makes many salespeople unwilling to mislead customers. This is especially true when sales are based on personal relationships. Salespeople can usually see that the personal codes of conduct which they demonstrate elsewhere in their lives contribute integrally to their success in sales.

A company that hires and sends out its sales representatives must make clear what it expects from them. The sales plan must be part of a larger, more comprehensive marketing strategy. The company must insist that whatever is promised be delivered, and that the interaction between sales and service is paramount. At no point does ethical decision-making become more important than in building the "moral cloth" of sales into the operation.

There is a reciprocal relationship between the individual and the business. Neither one can truly win if the reputation of either is harmed by the assumption that winning outweighs character.

A critic may say: If you are the only salesperson who places considerable weight on factors other than sheer volume, you will fall by the wayside. Similarly, a country which alone adheres to civilized rules of war among enemies who stop at nothing will probably not survive. Being moral is most praiseworthy, but being realistic is essential when the crunch comes.

Should salespeople abandon their scruples? Not at all. The moral requirement is that one move in the right direction, not that one be perfect. When more and more people move in the direction of "civilizing" sales practices, over time there will be considerable improvement. Even small improvements will eventually lead to broader progress in the long run, since each new level of improvement will become the standard against which future improvement must be measured.

Generally, a company's sales practices cannot be faulted as long as the company makes efforts continually to strengthen concern for the customer, clients, suppliers, the general public, and future generations. Virtually no one need be a martyr to the cause.

Without a motivation to adopt this broad, longer term perspective, unethical conduct feeds upon itself, whether in sales or other areas. Clearly, seeing the big picture from an ethical perspective allows businesses to better assess the meaning of their actions. In scientific research, if numerous practitioners were corrupt but little was done to remove their corruption, this would place pressure on the other researchers to likewise make use of inadequate data, accept support from interested parties, or sensationalize their findings. This sort of thing did happen in the Soviet Union a generation ago, when for a while bad biological science nearly drove out all good science. In our society, bad sales practices have tended to drive out the good ones, more for some products than for others. In general, unethical practices can, and often do, drive out ethical ones.

Why has this phenomenon so often been associated with sales? Part of the answer is that people have not adequately integrated the world of business into their lives as a whole. Centuries-old biases against commerce still hold sway, with the consequence that business is judged to be amoral. As we stated in Chapter Two, there is a widespread belief that business ought to follow its own rules. It is no wonder that sales practices, residing at the heart of business, should have suffered the most in this regard.

All too often, commerce lives up to our cynical expectations. We all pay a high price when we wink at unethical and amoral practices.

Further explanation for why there are so many Jim Smiths in this world lies in how we identify and teach values to youth. Parents can be poor role models. Unethical messages are sent in our advertising and the various media. However, the most important part of the explanation lies in the business systems that improperly reward sales efforts—that do not reward salespeople for placing integrity over commissions, that do not carefully evaluate the effects of the incentives in place, and that fail to integrate ethical business strategy with sales practices.

# CHAPTER FIVE

# Making Ethical Decisions

There are two possible models for ethical decision-making: (1) the "single moral value" approach and (2) moral pluralism.

When the first model is followed, every ethical decision boils down to determining how to apply a single value. An example of such a value is the "the greatest good for the greatest number." It belongs to the moral philosophy of *utilitarianism*. For utilitarians, every ethical question must be answered by determining what will bring about the greatest good for the greatest number of people. For example, should companies doing business in foreign countries offer bribes to officials in those countries? The utilitarian answer: Only if doing so will bring about the greatest good for the greatest number of people. Another question: Which sales practices should be followed by real estate agents such as Jim Smith (discussed in the previous chapter)? The utilitarian answer is that Jim Smith should follow whichever sales practices will bring about the greatest good for the greatest number of people.

When the second model for ethical decision-making is followed, ethical questions are *not* answered by appealing to a single basic moral value. According to moral pluralism, no such value exists. Instead, there are several basic moral values that must be balanced against each other when ethical decisions are made. How is this to be done? As you might suppose, the answer to this question is somewhat complicated; moral pluralism is a more complex model for ethical decision-making than the "single moral value" approach. However, in our opinion moral pluralism is the better model for ethical decision-making.

Distinguishing right from wrong is sometimes the easiest thing in the world, as, for example, when someone is tempted to pad an expense account. Doing such a thing in normal circumstances is wrong, and virtually everyone knows that it is wrong. In other cases, making an ethical decision may be extremely difficult, as in the case of a manager who must decide what to do with a long-time employee whose performance has become a problem for the company. In especially complex situations, such as corporate mergers or acquisitions where the interests of many individuals are involved, it may seem virtually impossible "to do the right thing for everyone."

One of the strengths of moral pluralism is that it helps to explain why making ethical decisions is sometimes extremely difficult. According to moral pluralism, as we said above, there is no single basic moral value, or principle, that can be appealed to, but instead there exist several different fundamental values that may conflict with one another. Making ethical decisions requires that an appropriate balance be found among these conflicting values. Potentially at least, this is a difficult task.

Of course, even in reference to a single basic moral value, ethical decision-making can be hard. Whatever the basic value is taken to be, it must be interpreted and applied in individual cases. Even doing this can be problematic. Many people do believe in a single value. (At least they say that they believe in a single value.) We have mentioned already the basic utilitarian value—"bringing about the greatest good for the greatest number." Other examples are "doing God's will on earth," "looking out for number one," and, in the limited context of business decisions, "maximizing the investments of stockholders." For each of these examples, difficult questions need to be asked: What will bring about the greatest good for the greatest number? What is God's will? How do we maximize stockholders' investments? What should we do to look out for ourselves and do a good job of it?

As though these questions were not difficult enough, moral pluralism requires that several different basic values be interpreted, applied, and balanced against each other.

We are the first to acknowledge that in committing ourselves to moral pluralism, we have compounded the difficulties to be found in ethical decision-making. Why have we done so? The answer to this question, at least, is simple and easy: No single basic moral value or principle by itself is satisfactory as a basis for making all important ethical decisions. No one principle works in every case.

## MORAL PLURALISM VS. UTILITARIANISM

Consider utilitarianism. Its basic decision-making principle can be stated as follows: Answer every ethical question by determining which course of action will bring about the greatest good for the greatest number of people over the longest period of time. Critics have been quick to point out that a lot can go wrong in following this principle. For example, utilitarianism is open to the charge that it neglects the moral rights or special needs of individuals and minorities. If the goal of our actions is always to look out for the *greatest number* of people, then the interests of individuals and minorities are left essentially unprotected in situations of conflict with the common good.

In a worst case scenario, utilitarians have no way to show, for example, that slavery is wrong. It is possible to imagine the existence of a hypothetical country where enslaving a few people helps to achieve the greatest good for the society as a whole. Another objectionable scenario might include a policy of "political triage" where the neediest individuals in a society are killed off because doing so benefits the group as a collective whole.

In defense of their view, utilitarians have attempted to show that policies such as slavery and killing people in need do not contribute to the greatest good. Among other bad effects, these policies would probably be demoralizing to society as a whole; if some people were made slaves or were sacrificed, then practically everyone in that society would probably worry about becoming slaves or being sacrificed. These bad effects would outweigh whatever good might be accomplished.

We are not satisfied with this utilitarian response because the moral value of individual rights ought to *stand by itself*, not be subordinated to the principle of the greatest good. Slavery is always a violation of individual rights, no matter what. Similarly, the moral value of justice, in the sense of helping the most those who are most in need, ought to stand by itself. We believe, further, that self-interest—when properly balanced against other moral values—should be given independent standing.

Thus, we are moral pluralists, committed to the view that ethical decision-making requires achieving a proper balance among the four different fundamental values—rights, justice, the common good, and self-interest. In what follows, we will define these values more precisely and discuss their application.

First, however, a caveat is in order. Ethical improvement in the workplace can occur at a number of different levels, some of which have little to do with moral theories or the controversies surrounding them. Moral pluralism is a controversial theory, just as utilitarianism is controversial. The same is true for all of the other theories that compete with these two, but which we do not have space enough to discuss here—theories based upon theology or upon the philosophies of Aristotle, Immanuel Kant, John Rawls, and others. Business people who are honest and concerned about the individuals they deal with can do a lot of good, regardless of whether they believe in moral pluralism. They can do that good even if they base their ethics on theology or are utilitarians, Kantians, or advocates of a "rights-based" moral philosophy. At the level of basic honesty and decency, the controversies surrounding these and other theories do not count.

The primary purpose of this book is to provide guidelines for ethical change in the workplace, not to win converts to moral pluralism. In our opinion, moral pluralism does provide the best overall guiding moral philosophy for ethical decision-making. However, it certainly is not the only moral philosophy that can benefit the workplace.

### MORAL PLURALISM

We have been referring to moral pluralism as though it were a single theory. That is not actually the case. Different versions of moral pluralism are possible depending upon which basic values are included. The version that we think best is committed to these four values:

Rights
Justice
The Common Good
Self-Interest

In earlier chapters, we discussed autonomy and the intrinsic worth of every human being. The four values listed above are not intended to be independent of these other two values, but instead to provide an analysis of them. As fundamental values, autonomy and the intrinsic worth of everyone need to be interpreted before they can serve as an effective guide to human conduct.

In Chapter One, the factory manager in our example was faced with closing a factory in a town where the factory was the mainstay of the local economy. Suppose we were to say to the manager: "Every human being has intrinsic worth; everyone should be treated as autonomous." Saying this would not help much in the manager's search for answers to all of the difficult questions that he or she faced. We would have said little more than that the interests of everyone concerned with the shutdown ought to be considered in some way— which is true and important, but constitutes only the first step in ethical decision-making.

A manager who believes that "business is amoral" or that corporations have obligations only to stockholders has not yet taken even that first step. Once the step is taken, numerous conflicts among people's interests come into play. Regardless of whether the factory closes or stays open, the interests of someone will be jeopardized— displaced employees, members of the community, stockholders, or future employees of the company.

What should the manager do? From the perspective of moral pluralism, the answer lies in finding an appropriate balance among the four basic values listed above. When the right balance is found, then and only then will proper recognition be given to the autonomy and intrinsic worth of all people.

How will the factory manager know when he or she has achieved the proper balance among the four values? To this question we can give no hard and fast answer. We can give guidelines. We can provide direction. But we cannot provide incontrovertibly correct ethical answers, nor can anyone else, in our opinion. Moral pluralism gives due recognition to a certain degree of openness, or indeterminacy, that is unavoidably present in ethical decision-making. Such openness is one of the strengths of moral pluralism. This is a subject to which we will return later in the chapter. We will also return a bit later to the example of the factory manager. Before doing that, we will describe further the four basic values of moral pluralism.

The world contains several billion people. Their interests, ambitions, hopes, fears, needs, and aspirations vary greatly. Some people are moral, some immoral. Some are law-abiding, some are criminal. Some are hardworking, some are indolent. Some people cooperate with their fellow human beings, others do not. Yet all have intrinsic worth. From a religious perspective, all people are precious in God's eyes.

Question: How can we sort and work through all the actual and potential differences in people, and still view each of them as possessors of intrinsic worth and autonomy? Moral pluralism provides a framework for giving an answer to this difficult question, or rather for acknowledging that no single, definitive answer is possible.

Only when taken together do the four values of moral pluralism express what is meant by a commitment to the intrinsic worth of all people as autonomous beings: Not only a commitment to protect the moral rights of every person; also, an acceptance of the obligation of justice to give help in response to greatest need; an acceptance of the obligation to make the world a better place overall; and a recognition of the unique value that each of us has to ourselves.

Writers, philosophers, theologians, and thinkers from many fields have for centuries discussed the concepts of rights, justice, the common good, and self-interest. This book is too short to enter far into those discussions, so we must content ourselves with somewhat rough and ready descriptions of the four basic values:

- The concept of rights is the idea that all people are in a fundamental way *equally valuable*. We ought to reach out to everyone on an equal basis.
- Justice means many different things. In the present sense, the concept of justice requires that we selectively help *those in most need*.
- The concept of the common good entails that sometimes the interests of a few will be subordinated to the interests of *the human race as a whole*. Sometimes, because we cannot be all things to all people, we should attempt simply to do the most good overall.
- Self-interest is the idea that sometimes and in some ways we should *put ourselves first*, not treat ourselves as one more face in the crowd.

At the present time in the United States and in much of the world, the sharpest controversies concerning rights are focused on their political dimension, on whether or not and to what extent the government should guarantee particular rights. The rights to life, liberty, and the pursuit of happiness are least controversial in this regard; virtually everyone believes that it is government's job to protect them. Rights to benefits such as medical care and welfare assistance are among the most controversial. The focus of this book is on the *moral*, not the political, dimension of rights—insofar as they can be separated. Discussion of the political dimension of rights would take us too far afield. In the workplace, the basic idea of rights is "equal protection."

The moral value of justice, in the sense of helping people in proportion to their needs, enjoins us to give special help to the most needy. In the workplace, if managers were to consider only the concept of rights, they would treat all employees in a wholly impartial fashion as regards such factors as race, gender, age, poverty, or affluence. However, managers should not be wholly impartial in these matters, but instead sometimes should give special consideration to individuals or groups who have special needs, such as employees who have suffered from discrimination based on race, gender, physical handicap, or sexual preference. Similarly, when a factory must be closed, managers ought to give special consideration to those who are hurt the most by the closing; again, complete impartiality is not appropriate.

The moral value of the common good enjoins us to look toward larger and larger wholes. In the workplace, if managers go too far in their efforts to help victims of discrimination or anyone who has suffered deprivation, then the managers' actions may undermine the common good—or threaten the rights of other individuals. But sometimes a manager will find it necessary to forgo providing both equal protection to all and special benefits to those in greatest need in order to achieve the common good by strengthening the corporation as a whole; this might be the case when a struggling company closes its weakest factories but does not have the resources to help displaced workers. Management is doing what it can to avoid bankruptcy, which would be harmful to the company as a whole and probably to the society of which it is a part.

A word of caution: What we have just said is oversimplified, a universal danger in discussions of ethics. For example, helping victims of discrimination is a good thing to do not only because the individuals may be in special need of help. Helping them will likely contribute in its own way to the common good and may in addition help to protect their rights. The points we have made are intended to illustrate just a few of the important ways that values conflict.

Moral sensitivity lies in knowing how far to go in each of several different directions.

The only "principle of principles" in moral pluralism is the requirement that a balance be found among the four values. In every ethical decision, each of the values must at least *be considered*.

Someone who says: "I care nothing for rights," or "I care nothing for helping people in need," or "In this case, the good of society does not matter at all," or "You should never think of yourself but only those whom you serve," is wrong. None of the values can ever be totally disregarded.

In finding an appropriate balance of values, self-interest must be balanced against all three of the "other-directed values" (rights, justice, the common good). At the same time, each of the other-directed values must be balanced against the others. These two dimensions to the "balancing act" prescribed by moral pluralism cannot neatly be distinguished from each other because a person's self-interest cannot neatly be distinguished from the interests of other people. For example, if you act to protect rights in general, you are also helping to protect your own rights; you are benefiting both self and others. The same may be true regarding helping people in need and acting for the sake of the common good. Nevertheless, the overall thrust of actions directed toward rights, justice, and the common good is usually toward helping other people more than oneself. Acting for the sake of self-interest typically does not involve concern for basic ethical values as much as it does concern for one's own career, business, hobbies, or personal life.

One of the ways to become better at making moral decisions is to practice making them. Also, it helps to pay close attention to the moral decisions of others. It helps to talk and act in ways that are described by objective observers as more empathetic in terms of individual and group need.

Moral decision-making is an art, not a science. Two people can be equally well informed, sensitive, and experienced and still end up in disagreement. When such disagreements occur, an external third party can guide us in finding a better solution. Even when there is no disagreement, ethical decision-making in the workplace requires an openness to public scrutiny and review. A peer review system is an effective strategy for providing accountability. Such a system allows management to better assess the ethical components and effects of corporate decisions.

## EXAMPLES FOR DISCUSSION

These examples illustrate the need in ethical decision-making to find an appropriate balance among conflicting values. While they may appear simple on the surface, it is in these everyday dilemmas that most of us have the opportunity to sharpen our ethical decision-making skills for the larger issues we may well face in the work-place.

## Example 1

You, George, have to make a big sale in order to meet a quota before the end of the month in a computer store where you work. Uninformed customers want to buy software for their computers. One of your customers is a determined and naive man who wants to buy a particular brand of desktop publishing software for his office computer. He wants it to work in his laptop as well. He describes a number of programs that he currently has loaded on the laptop, all of which he considers essential.

In most such cases you would ask the individual to bring his laptop to your store in order to make sure that the memory capacity is adequate for the program. You do not offer this option to your present customer but instead yield to his impatient demand that he purchase the "best" desktop publishing software available for a contract he is completing. He has read about the brand in question and that is what he wants. You are reasonably certain that he does not have the equipment needed to start the program. You mention once that you could sell him a different program that would do the job he needs for less money, but he is not interested. You do not object, but sell to him what he wants, without making much of the fact that he may have to buy a "few more things" to make it work.

It is close to the end of the month, and your sale of the software will put you over the top. By the time the man either returns the software or buys more equipment, you will have received temporary credit for the sale. This sale will keep the sales manager off your back while you make new sales. You are not positive the customer can return the program, but he is so certain regarding what he wants and impatient with your advice that you skip discussing this point. Next month you may have to make up for this sale, but you can think about that later.

You have met your needs and satisfied your customer's immediate concern. What should you have done differently, if anything? Did you balance self-interest and the interest of your customer sufficiently in arriving at the decision to sell? If you submitted a report of this sale to an outside review, what would others say about your efforts?

## Example 2

You have completed the interview of a woman who has applied for a position in your firm as a design engineer, and you have decided not to hire her. For the interview, she brought with her a computer disk containing information on her recent work. She showed it to you briefly on your computer, and you found it to be most interesting and potentially valuable to your firm. You would like to have had time to study the specifics of the information on her disk. As it happens, you now have a chance to do just that because she has forgotten the disk, leaving it behind in your computer. It would be an easy matter for you to copy it before calling the woman to tell her that she should come back to pick it up.

If you were to do this, there is almost no chance that you would ever be caught. Moreover, as far as you know, the woman who owns the disk would not be hurt in any substantial way by your theft of the information, while you have reason to believe that you and your company would benefit significantly. At the same time, you also know that the owner of the disk would not voluntarily give you the information even if you were to hire her. You do not want to do so because you have another candidate for the job whom you judge will fit much better into your operation. What should you do?

In any civilized society, there are strong prohibitions against theft; laws and moral rules against stealing tell us that it is wrong regardless of who will benefit and who will be harmed by the theft. Such rules are needed for the protection of individual rights and for the sake of the common good. Therefore, if in the above example you "act on principle," you will not steal the information. A person who adheres strictly to professional codes of conduct is acting on principle. Such a person does not lie, cheat, steal, or in any way violate the basic moral rules that are a part of civilized life.

Could you justify copying the disk as supporting your company's increased knowledge, as a higher order of value than the rule against theft? If you were to copy the disk, could you sincerely assert that the principle you were acting on is promoting the greatest good for the greatest number?

Sometimes rules that protect individual rights should be broken for the sake of the common good or to help people in need, but this example does not appear to be such a case, partly because the rule against theft plays such an important role in civilized society. An unusually strong reason is needed to justify stealing. For example, most people believe, correctly we think, that, when other resources fail, it is morally permissible to steal a loaf of bread when doing so is necessary to feed a starving child. The child's need is as great as can be imagined, while the harm done to civilized society by the theft would be relatively slight.

## Example 3

James has recently graduated with a degree in business administration. He is offered two jobs, one with a building supplies firm and one with a tobacco company. Work conditions, benefits, and prospects for advancement are similar for the two jobs, but the tobacco company is offering a significantly higher salary. James has recently gotten married and plans to have a family. Which job should he take?

The primary moral conflict here is between James's self-interest, on the one hand, and the common good, on the other hand. The job with the tobacco company will do *him* more good, while the job with the building supplies company will presumably benefit society to a much greater extent. His moral choice would appear to be relatively straightforward: He should take the job with the building supplies company. However, to make a good decision, he should obtain information pertaining to such matters as the record of the building supplies company regarding pollution control and treatment of minorities and women.

At the present time, prospective employees may feel reluctant to ask ethical questions in employment interviews. It is our hope that in the future this situation will change. Certainly both employers and prospective employees readily and sensitively should ask ethical questions.

## Example 4

You have been asked to inflate sales figures "just this once" by the manager of your division, who says that his job is on the line and that he will never ask you to do it again. You would like to help the man because he is hardworking, fair, and kind to you, and has always acted responsibly as far as you know.

This is another example involving moral rules, where acting on principle requires that you refuse to lie on the man's behalf. Rules against lying play an essential role in the protection of individual rights as well as in promoting the common good. In terms of justice (as we are using the word) you ought to "help the most those who most need help." The manager of your division does need help because he is about to lose his job, but that is not a sufficiently strong reason to justify lying on his behalf.

You will likely feel some remorse about your inability to help him, but you can instead offer your support by making positive statements about his leadership to those who manage him. You can take responsibility for whatever part your actions or failure to act may have played in the reduced sales. If you lie, however, you put many people on the line, including yourself. Even if you believe that the man has been given an unfair sales target or that the company employing him is impossible to work for, taking steps to inflate the sales figures is wrong. You must define the issues as you see them— consider fairness, the marketplace, the skills of yourself and colleagues, the leadership of the manager and the requirements of the company. After making those analyses, tackle any and all of these issues in a responsible and sensitive manner. These are the proper ways to resolve concerns you may have.

## Example 5

Mary has single-handedly set the stage for establishing a new branch office in Alaska for her New York firm. She has met with the pertinent people in Alaska and gotten their written agreement as needed on all the essential matters except, as she discovers once she is back in New York, for one thing. She has forgotten to get an authorized signature for releasing for shipment the contents of a warehouse whose lease her company is taking over. Getting this signature is the least important matter that she had to attend to while in Alaska, and in fact is really only a formality. She knows that she can get the signature mailed to her by the following week, but that will be too late to present as documentation for the new branch office at a corporate meeting the next morning in New York. Because her boss is a stickler for details, she knows that not having the signature could cause a crucial delay and hurt her career. She is confident that forging the signature herself will hurt no one's interests.

In this example, it is possible that the requirements for acting on principle—for following strictly the rules that society needs to protect rights and advance the common good—are not strong enough to outweigh the benefits, to Mary especially, that forgery would bring. Is a consideration of her self-interest strong enough to outweigh other ethical concerns? If she does sign the document, what else need she do, if anything, to improve the ethics of the decision? Are there any other actions she could take that will help her respond to the concerns she believes are there? Are there any issues strictly inside the company? How can she address the matter and still succeed at her meeting the next morning? Should she sign and wait until after the meeting to address the additional issues? What else should she consider in making her decision?

## Example 6

Mike, who is in charge of product planning for his firm, meets Cynthia at a convention. She is his counterpart at a rival company. After chatting with her, he makes two discoveries: first, that he is attracted to her, and second, that his own company clearly has the inside track on new products for the coming year. He is in a position to do his own firm a lot of harm if he were even to hint to her what some of his company's plans are. Neither is married. If he asks her for a date, particularly before the new product line is released, he would be violating his company's code of conduct. At the same time, he trusts himself absolutely not to give away any company secrets. He judges that no harm would result if he violates his company's code of conduct, except possibly by the example he would set. If he were to date Cynthia before the release of his company's new product line, he would be discreet. Probably no one would know about it.

Should he act on principle or should he put his own interest, and Cynthia's, first? Who might be affected by his actions? How should he weigh opportunity for himself against responsibilities to his company? If he were to date her, what concrete steps could he take to ensure that his actions would be discreet?

As you think about these cases, bear in mind what we said earlier, that ethics is an art, not a science. There is often room for disagreement between two individuals who possess the same high degree of moral integrity, are morally sensitive, and have all pertinent information. While the lack of precision and certainty may be frustrating, it is also true that one of the things that makes ethical decision-making interesting and even profound is just this room for equally ethical individuals to see matters somewhat differently.

# CHAPTER SIX

# The Office Climate

There is a German saying to the effect that two things make life worth living: *lieben und arbeiten,* to love and to work. If work is to make a positive contribution to people's lives, then certain conditions must be met. It would be ideal if every aspect of the workplace could be arranged so as to improve the quality of life. If this were done, the likelihood would be increased that a company would be maximally profitable. But, also, it ought to be done for its own sake insofar as this is possible.

What follows is a list of the major respects in which the workplace may have an impact on people's lives:

- *The physical setting*—lighting, temperature, air quality, desks, chairs, workstations; accessibility to files, copying machines, and rest rooms; privacy or lack of privacy; proximity to daycare facilities; food services; facilities for exercise.
- *The psychological setting*—feelings of mastery and confidence; levels of stress; feelings of camaraderie with other employees or the absence of such feelings; expectations as to performance, personal habits, and appearance.
- *The connection between work and personal life*—use of screening tests such as polygraphs and personality profiles; loyalty to the company; prohibitions against public criticism of the company or the absence thereof; the extent to which a company contributes to or restricts an employee's social life.
- *The "culture" of a corporation*—that which is distinctive about the way that a company does business; its goals and values.

## THE PHYSICAL SETTING

A fundamental question that an employer must ask is: Do employees have the resources to do their jobs? Employees who have at hand all necessary equipment and supplies and are working in a comfortable work environment will look forward to work each day. Under those circumstances, most employees will do the very best work they can and remain loyal to the company.

The physical layout of an office or other workplace has a great deal to do with how people behave in that environment. The convenient location of essential equipment and supplies, desks that are matched to the types of work being done, the selection of lamps, chairs, tables, even pictures—all must be taken into account and made appropriate to their users. Temperature, air quality, and noise levels must be taken into account. The physical arrangement in which people find themselves either encourages them or discourages them from including the "little extras" that spell success or failure for a corporation's goals. Management's commitment to the well-being of employees is on display in the workplace setting.

One way to increase the probability that employees will enjoy work and do their best is to solicit their suggestions about improving the physical setting of the workplace. A specialist in ergonomics or a safety engineer might be helpful, especially in workplaces that are potentially hazardous. Employees will most likely repay management's consideration with a greater enthusiasm for their jobs.

## THE PSYCHOLOGICAL SETTING

*Theory Z: How American Business Can Meet the Japanese Challenge* by William G. Ouchi was a revelation to American managers a decade ago. Ouchi compared "Type Z" companies, typified by successful Japanese firms, with "Type A" companies, typified by American firms. The most striking contrast was psychological. Ouchi noted that people felt much different when working for Type Z corporations. People felt less stress, deeper camaraderie, more security, and a greater sense of belonging to the company. They felt many of the same feelings of belonging that people experience within their own families. Overall, they felt better. "The employees at Company Z manifest much better emotional well-being than their counterparts at Company A."[1] As a result, Type Z companies exhibited much less job turnover at all levels.

Why did the employees feel better at Type Z companies? The answer that Ouchi gives is complex, but none of it will surprise readers of this book. Nor will any of it be surprising to readers of other recent books that describe the "new management" philosophy based upon ideas that go back at least to the early 1950s when W. Edwards Deming went to Japan to teach his management philosophy to key Japanese business leaders. Deming advocated then, and continues to promote to this day, a nonauthoritarian approach to management. Managers should motivate not through fear but through respect. In place of constantly looking over an employee's shoulder, checking and testing for the "correct" behavior, managers should give employees broad responsibility for producing high-quality products that meet needs of consumers.

Deming's ideas are echoed and elaborated upon by a growing number of contemporary management experts.

"In the worst form of supervision, the supervisor is overseeing, constantly criticizing, not just building resentment but making things progressively worse."[2] Pride of workmanship should be used as a prime motivational factor. In place of chastising workers for doing a poor job, they should be encouraged to identify areas of difficulty and given extensive training on how to do a better job. As much as possible, they should monitor and correct their own errors. "The leader asks people what they want to do—what they think they should do—to solve their own problems."[3] Managers must enhance the interaction between achieving short-term goals and building the future.

Like all new ideas, the pioneering concepts of Deming and others who have become known as advocates of the "quality imperative" doubtless need to be tested, modified, and corrected. Ideas that have worked well for Japanese companies in the context of Japanese culture will need to be modified to fit American cultural practices, or our cultural practices may themselves need to be modified.

The first rule of the "new management" is to treat everyone well. No one has yet said the last word on what it means to treat everyone well. Let us return for a moment to *Theory Z*.

Not everyone feels comfortable in the Type Z corporation described by Ouchi. For one thing, such corporations require high levels of participation by all employees. Upon joining a Type Z company, the new employee "drops most of his communal ties and participates almost exclusively in his work-related groups."[4] Those who can adjust to this organization will likely find work conditions ideal. Conversely, those who cannot fit in or feel uncomfortable in this environment will probably find that other styles of management are more suitable and that such styles can be equally effective in demonstrating respect to employees.

Type Z corporations may ask and expect too much from their employees. Do the new styles of management convey this excessive expectation? From a moral point of view, we must ask the basic question: How much can a company rightly expect from its employees? We return to this question in Chapter Nine.

To a considerable extent, the level of what is expected from employees is beyond the control of any one individual corporation. Levels of performance must measure up to world standards if a company is to compete worldwide. In the global economy of the 1990s, almost all successful companies must compete internationally or be prepared to do so. Nevertheless, a point of diminishing returns exists in that expecting too much from employees will yield lower overall returns to the company than would have been achieved if expectations had been lower. Excessive demands will produce failure, exhaustion, or at least resentment. Some room is required for individual discretion and judgment.

Will managers attempt to squeeze one more ounce of effort from an employee? At that point, the decision should be guided by respect for the worker first and company profitability second. Such a path is likely to lead to more consistent performance and, thus, increased profits.

## THE CONNECTION BETWEEN WORK AND PERSONAL LIFE

American companies have frequently taken a shortsighted view of what it means for employees to be "loyal to the company." Managers of many major corporations have believed that a loyal employee will never publicly criticize the company on ethical, legal, or practical grounds. However, many of these same companies could have saved themselves from much expense and embarrassment if they had encouraged and actively supported employees to speak out about their concerns, no matter how sensitive, within the confines of the company and had seen such comments as opportunities both to improve understanding and, where appropriate, to make changes to address the concerns raised. A commitment to ethical conduct and its evaluation is essential for any corporation concerned about the effects of its actions. There is no greater loyalty than to bring to the attention of management potential or actual problem spots.

No distinction should be drawn between freedom of speech in one's personal life and freedom of speech in one's life as an employee. As with the free speech granted to Americans, consequences are attached to slanderous statements. In addition, employees may be restricted from disclosing proprietary information, e.g., competitive strategies, plans and development of products and services, and personnel information. Companies need to articulate rights and responsibilities in regard to speech. These can be written into company policy statements, but it is even more important that managers be committed to the open exchange of ideas.

Another area where corporations have sometimes taken a short-sighted view concerns invasions of employees' privacy. Of particular concern to us is the use of tests such as polygraphs and personality profiles. Our stand is not that the use of such tests is always wrong, but that it is *too often* wrong and usually counterproductive in the long run. Such tests generate mistrust. They ignore individuality. They predict general consequences based on statistical analysis of traits. The results often do not indicate how an individual will respond in a new setting.

Such tests are least problematic from an ethical perspective when they are used as preliminary screenings only, to prepare an interviewer to ask the right questions. However, an employer may say: "With our high turnover among employees, we cannot afford a more personal approach to hiring." Our response: The high turnover is the basic problem; that ought to be addressed first. Another employer may say: "Pilfering of supplies has gotten out of hand. We have two thousand employees, so we must have a quick way to screen them for honesty." Our reply: Written tests by themselves cannot give you enough information to evaluate the honesty or dishonesty of any one employee.

Another area is safety on the job. The most important moral requirement here is full disclosure. All information about hazards, safety equipment, and possible long-term risks in the workplace must be disclosed. While employers cannot totally eliminate risks to health in the workplace, a policy of full disclosure does allow for informed consent. Someone may object that full disclosure does not go far enough because many employees are "coerced" by economic realities into taking or keeping a job regardless of workplace hazards. There is some truth to this claim.

How should a corporation dedicated to ethical behavior respond? There is no way it can promise total elimination of *all* health risks; all workplaces have hazards of one sort or another. Some are quite minimal, such as slipping on damp tiles in the rest room, while others are potentially lethal, such as working with underground mining machinery. Reduction of health hazards will in the long run result in savings for most companies, but there is no guarantee that this will happen. A company has the moral responsibility to eliminate as many hazards as possible on an active and ongoing basis.

Where the immediate and total elimination of a particular risk to health is prohibitively expensive, the morally correct course of action for an individual company is to move in the direction of greater safety and full disclosure to its employees. A company that does this and also advertises its changes will "nudge" the entire industry toward reform. If all or most companies attempted to be "better than the competition," in a relatively short time health dangers could be significantly reduced. Recognition of the problem and moving in the right direction are essential.

## THE "CULTURE" OF A CORPORATION

We cannot stress too much the need for an explicit reference to ethical values in a company's "vision statement." Every company stands for something. Why not make what the company stands for explicitly ethical? Public statements that define the corporation's ethical standards increase the probability of such behavior. In turn, the company is saved from the expenses of unethical conduct.

At heart, ethical behavior is a kind of mind-set, an attitude that includes respect for all persons and an endeavor to find an appropriate balance among important values. These ought to be an explicit part of a company's vision statement: We treat customers well by producing and standing behind the best XYZ; we make our contribution to bettering the world by providing ABC. For all companies, Deming has said it well: "A company exists to provide goods and services which help improve the standard of living of mankind."[5]

At any given time, a company will necessarily be following specific procedures for the manufacture of its products and the provision of its services. As well, a company may have in place specific guidelines for enhancing its ethical conduct toward employees—regarding office furnishings, hiring and promotion procedures, and so on. All of these procedures and guidelines need to be open to modification if better ways are found to manufacture products or to treat employees well.

In today's global marketplace, corporations more and more recognize the need for specialized services and for listening to and fulfilling customers' specific needs. Success depends upon listening well. Such a focus requires a painstaking assessment of what the company does well and what it does not do well. Some companies will master the design, manufacture, and marketing of products with extremely short turnaround times, such as personal computers. The resultant fast turnover of products becomes part of the corporate culture, "how we do business." Other companies' products have long turnaround times, or they take many risks in marketing new products, or fewer risks, or they endeavor to meet people's existing needs, or they create products first and then educate people to want them. Needless to say, there is no right or wrong among any of these options.

Similarly, companies can "specialize" internally in meeting employee needs. Within a wide range of corporate policies and structures, there are no absolute rights and wrongs. For example, where Company X can gain a reputation for providing excellent day care for working parents, Company Y can be known to offer optical and dental care. Another company might offer flexible vacations. However, not all companies can or should put equal effort into all of these spheres, or into programs for retraining laid-off workers, or into finding special niches for older employees, or into including exercise rooms, health food in cafeterias, or preventive medical checkups. There are both practical limits and limits imposed by the needs of the employees. For example, child care is not an issue for a company of older employees, nor is elder care necessarily an issue for a newly formed youthful enterprise.

As part of "how we do business," every company should be dedicated to treating everyone well. This dedication should be a part of stated company policy, a prominent part of what the company stands for in the eyes of its employees, customers, suppliers, competitors, and the world at large.

## NOTES

1.   William G. Ouchi, *Theory Z* (New York: Avon Books, 1981), p. 183.

2.   Rafael Aguayo, *Dr. Deming: The American Who Taught the Japanese About Quality* (New York: Fireside, 1990), p. 176.

3.   Joseph H. Boyett and Henry P. Conn, *Workplace 2000: The Revolution Reshaping American Business* (New York: Dutton, 1991), p. 158.

4.   Ouchi, *Theory Z*, pp. 167-68.

5.   W. Edwards Deming as quoted in Aguayo, *Dr. Deming*, p. 129.

# CHAPTER SEVEN

# The Process of Achieving Ethical Change

This chapter describes strategies for implementing behavior change. The strategies apply to ethical change as well as other types of change. These strategies can be used by managers to change the behavior of employees and by individual employees to change their own behavior.

Optimal conditions for initiating and then maintaining organizational change depend upon a company-wide commitment to positive strategies of change described below and a commitment to building the infrastructure of the organization upon basic tenets of ethical decision-making (Chapter Five). Successful, enduring personal change in the workplace depends on how well the organization supports, enhances, and then preserves individual change. This link between the individual and his or her workplace needs to be clearly understood.

The best work settings are those that make positive change possible for individuals, while individuals, in turn, affect positively the settings in which they work. "As I change, you change, and in turn, your change changes me." Undertaking ethical change offers the possibility for enriching our everyday world.

The processes for achieving ethical change require understanding, a systematic approach, commitment and cooperation, and hard work. There are no shortcut methods.

## BELIEFS THAT IMPEDE ETHICAL CHANGE

Changing behavior, whether one's own or that of someone else, is not easy. When the desired change is toward behavior that is more ethical, there are special problems. Indeed, so many impediments exist that some people believe that alteration of personal ethics is impossible or nearly impossible. At the same time, in contrast, numerous popular books and tapes attempt to convey the message that behavior of all kinds can be changed easily, including our ethical sensitivities and actions.

We begin by examining beliefs that may inhibit the process of ethical change.

1. *The belief that merely understanding behavior is enough to change it.*

Behavior change requires much more than insight into what needs to be changed. An understanding of the benefits that derive from changing either ourselves or others, though important, is not enough to bring about significant changes. If it were, the need for most of the popular self-help books would disappear! Nor is it enough to have good understanding, or insight, into the causes of our behavior. Knowing and doing are two different things.

An unrealistic outlook based on assuming we know how to change can keep us from doing the hard work necessary for actual ethical change to occur. This work includes designing or redesigning work settings, creating incentive systems, and modifying patterns of interaction among personnel.

2. *The belief that ethical values cannot be changed.*

This belief is the opposite of the one we just discussed. "You can't change character," people sometimes say. They assume that change in ethical behavior is impossible to any significant degree. They believe that once set, personality and the values reflected in it cannot change.

On the contrary, we can understand "character" in terms of personality traits. A trait can usefully be thought of as a group of individual behaviors to which we attach meaning in terms of a label that describes the usual ways in which an individual can be expected to behave. A personality trait is not an individual behavior but a name for a cluster of behaviors which have something in common. For example, being shy can be described in terms of specific acts of the individual—eye contact, posture, and frequency of conversation. Similarly, we can understand honesty in terms of behaviors such as making and keeping promises, telling the truth, and paying debts punctually.

To change a personality trait is to change a significant number of the individual behaviors that define it. When personality traits are understood to be more than the composite of single, clearly identifiable individual behaviors, we may feel helpless to do anything about them. Such helplessness is an impediment to success in changing ethical behavior. Individual behaviors, our own and those of others, can be changed.

Still, there is no getting around the fact that personality traits are difficult to change. A large number of individual behaviors define any one personality trait. Moreover, these behaviors occur across virtually all settings: at home, at work, in public places, in private circumstances, and so on. When we correctly label a person as having integrity or honesty, we do so on the basis of expecting the person to exhibit predictably honest and principled actions in many different settings.

Is it possible to change a large number of interrelated individual behaviors? Most of us believe that it is when we think in terms of concrete examples, as for example in the case of a typist overcoming errors. A new manager can learn to run a good meeting. More generally, a passive person can learn to say "no" assertively across settings. In each of these cases, change involves progressively larger numbers of discrete individual actions. Accordingly, this is the model that we employ regarding ethical change: Character and the values that reflect it can be understood as "summary statements" for a large number of "small" individual behaviors. These behaviors are preserved to a significant degree by the consequences of our acts. Change strategies, therefore, must focus on the consequences of individual actions across settings.

If we give sufficient support for the small changes a person makes, over time these small changes tend to redefine "who the person is." In turn, the person's values will change in support of the new collection of actions that demonstrate his or her character: honesty, integrity, respect for others.

3. *A belief that we should not "force our values on others."*

As a society, we have an ambivalent attitude toward ethical behavior, especially in the world of business. We do believe in ethics and we admire those who practice it. But we also are as likely to believe that advocating ethical behavior or ethical improvement makes us appear judgmental, uncompromising, or unrealistic.

Part of the problem has to do with the belief that ethical decision-making leaves no room for compromise or the possibility of disagreement among informed and sensitive individuals. On the contrary, the essence of ethical decision-making is finding a balance among conflicting values with room for compromise and rational disagreement. Moral pluralism, discussed in Chapter Five, is a model for ethical decision-making that emphasizes the need to balance conflicting values.

Another part of the problem lies in the belief that business is, and ought to be, amoral. In reality, as discussed in Chapter Two, business is subject to the same moral rules that are other spheres of life.

An additional part of the problem lies in a faulty assessment of the extent to which advocating ethical change in the workplace addresses matters that are personal in nature. No one wants to invade privacy. Hence, management tends to review only the technical skills of the individual. It is important to realize that the overall manner in which employees conduct themselves in the workplace just as appropriately can be reviewed by management. We can each be held to moral or ethical standards in the workplace that are even higher than our usual standards. This is not an invasion of our privacy or of our right to be our own person. Once the individual enters the workplace, he or she makes a commitment to uphold the standards of the workplace. Both interpersonal and personal aspects of a person's workplace conduct, as well as technical skill, are part of the right and duty of managers to shape and direct.

4. *The belief that advocating ethical change involves large risks.*

Of course, change of any kind involves risk. In our opinion, supporting ethical change in the workplace actually involves fewer risks than a great many other types of change. Still, it is understandable that "defending what is right" may appear to jeopardize our jobs, our families, or our security.

In many situations, we overestimate risk because the behaviors we need to exhibit are novel and uncomfortable. There can be risk in ethical actions, but when we approach them sincerely and assume that the other person is just as ready to act with integrity as we are, we reduce the risks. When we stand up for what we believe, rarely will we have to pursue a course of action where the only choices are between extremes. Not every injustice in the workplace requires that we quit our jobs.

The model for ethical decision-making described in Chapter Five will help you approach troublesome situations in a way that poses relatively few risks. Look for evidence that those with whom you have disagreements or conflicts embrace at least some of the basic values of moral pluralism, which, as you may recall, involves finding a proper balance among rights, justice, the common good, and self-interest. Finding common ground when involved in conflict is critical to achieving better understanding and, more importantly, conflict resolution.

Keep in mind that two individuals, both of whom are ethical, can adopt the same basic values while assigning to them different degrees of importance in specific situations. Argue for your own position by saying, for example: "I'm glad that in this case we both believe in protecting rights and helping people in need. But let me suggest why I believe we need to do more for those in need than we are presently doing."

The processes of demonstrating ethical conduct and defending one's actions need not be threatening to others, or to oneself. There are many ways to create a more ethical environment. Flexibility, listening to what is presented, and inviting others to find challenging and effective new ways of approaching problems are all part of the opportunity.

We advise taking relatively small steps—addressing individual and/or organizational behaviors one by one. The potential impact one can have differs at the various levels of influence. The relative risks differ as well. For example, an office manager may encourage her employees to get involved in community service. A supervisor may invite his employees to participate in monthly planning meetings. At a regional sales meeting, a sales manager may speak out about the need to reassess incentive plans because they unfairly reward his unit without any recognition for the efforts of other departments. A senior manager may tell her CEO that senior managers are mishandling the human side of a recent acquisition and have thereby failed to provide clear leadership. In each succeeding example just described, the risks for confrontation and disfavor increase somewhat as the issues involve wider constituent groups. Nevertheless, the more responsibility assigned to an individual, the greater the need for actions or comments that have the potential to clarify and resolve ethical issues. In each instance, taking relatively small steps increases the likelihood that further progress will follow. These examples are about the common good, fairness, honesty, and justice. They are not about achieving extraordinary levels of moral character. It is in ordinary activities that ethical action is most frequently required.

5. *The belief that labels accurately describe individuals.*

A fifth and significant impediment to ethical change has to do with the use of labels in describing or referring to people. If we attach certain labels, such as "shy" or "a bore," we will impede the process of change. However, if we attach other labels, such as "bright" or "a team player," we *may* enhance the process. The role of labels in ethical behavior change is complex; the main point to keep in mind is that customary ways that labels are used almost always hinder rather than help the process of change. In any case, labels color our view. When undertaking to manage people most effectively or to change ourselves or others, we are usually better off not attaching labels at all.

It is easy to attach labels to others that do not describe them accurately—with bad consequences to them, to us, and to the organizations of which they are a part. At the same time, in order to bring about ethical change most effectively, our goal is not simply to attach the most "accurate" labels. Labels of any kind can draw our attention away from the specific behaviors where change needs to occur. Yet, the use of "positive" labels, such as "a leader," for example, can help in positively changing a person's ethical behavior— as long as we are not taken in by our own labels. We must see others for what they are.

The use of labels of all kinds is widespread because attaching labels to people's actions is a handy and efficient method of grouping individual actions into an understandable whole. Labeling is inevitable. Others know us by what we say and what we do. Over time, our actions take on a certain predictability and offer a quick way for others to describe us—shy, talkative, earnest, "the life of the party," aggressive, a bore, a leader, and so on. Once such labels are attached, others usually believe that they know how to interact meaningfully with us. In a sense, we have become our labels.

It is often easier to begin interacting comfortably with people we have just met if we can first observe and then label their interactions with others. We attach meaning to a person's social behavior. Based on our past experience with similar cases, we anticipate how a new person will act. In reality, the labels we attach to the new person describe only a small portion of the skills and actions that the person might demonstrate. The use of negative labels is especially problematic; we discuss them in the next section.

6. *A belief that negative labels reflect "who the person is."*

Negative labels are often ascribed too quickly to others. For example, at work we might label a person as "lazy" because that person always arrives late to meetings and once there does not participate. Labels are summary statements intended to describe what is observed, as we said. However, they go beyond simple description when they summarize "who the person is"—in this case, lazy. In reality, whether our experience is quite limited as it usually is, or more extensive, we often do not know "who the person is."

The disservice we have done is perhaps greater than we realize, because this inaccurate generalization is likely to follow a person everywhere. From the perspective of management, we have made change appear to be more difficult to achieve than it actually is. For example, it may well not be laziness at all that needs to be overcome, but merely a few specific behaviors.

All too often, the use of labels such as "lazy" is based on a small sample of behaviors. Then, once the label is attached, different people will read into it different meanings depending upon their individual experiences in the past with "lazy people." Thus the significance attached to the original behaviors—in our original example, lateness and a failure to participate—may end up being *much* weightier than it should be.

It is harder to change laziness than to improve punctuality. Laziness is a trait of personality, after all. A manager or a peer may give up before getting started. This is one reason that inaccurate, negative labeling can be counterproductive. A second reason is that people too readily believe the labels that have been applied to them. If you call a tardy person lazy once too often, the person may fulfill your characterization. Regardless, the individual's potential has been reduced.

Furthermore, we have injured ourselves by reducing our ability to see the real person. We stop responding to the person, and begin responding to the label no matter what the person does. He or she is judged to be "lazy inside." We say, "Oh, that's not George. That's just a front. He's working hard to finish that report only because he knows we're watching." George has been hurt and we have been hurt. He must overcome a deficit that does not exist, or would not have existed. We must overcome our own misunderstanding as well. We have limited our view of George's potential, treating him quite differently than we would want to be treated. Perhaps most important, we must repair the injustice of what we have done.

We tend to act toward others in a manner that complies with our expectations. If people have been assigned negative labels, we will ask less of them. We may deprive the workplace of potentially valuable contributions when we don't assign such people important projects. We may not even consider them when assigning new projects.

7. *A belief that positive labels reflect "who the person is."*

Negative labels cause the most problems in limiting the approach to behavior change. But even ascribing positive general characteristics can be problematic. One reason is that doing so can lead us to expect from others more than they are able to achieve. We will have set them up to fail.

On the other hand, if we label someone as potentially "better than he or she is," and we are realistic, we are acting with sensitivity regarding change. One of the requirements for any process of change to occur is to set up expectations that produce the change and reward small steps toward the goal. Ascribing positive attributions can help in beginning that process.

Seeing the possibilities in others is essential for effective management, as long as we are not misled. The strongest base for building positive change occurs when we see "who a person is" by what the person actually does, not by what we wish he or she did. First, we must correctly observe others, then support them in exceeding current performance.

8. *A belief that who I say I am is as important as what I do.*

As well as mislabeling others, people may label themselves inadvertently and inaccurately through the language they use. We have all encountered "the grouch," someone who constantly complains about others, yet demonstrates by his actions that he in fact cares for others. The words he speaks tell one story, his actions tell quite another. He uses "grouchy language" and takes pride in calling himself a grouch. But if the word "grouchy" were replaced with "caring," we may well be closer to describing who he is and the effect he has on others.

Most of us learn from others what to call ourselves. Children learn to call themselves bullies, babies, shy, or awkward. As adults we sometimes preempt the ability of others to attach a negative label to us by giving them one to use when thinking about us. When the label we offered becomes effective, determining how others respond to us, we sometimes then, illogically, are doubly assured that we can be nothing else. On the other hand, if we have tried to avert criticism by labeling ourselves with positive words that we do not believe, we may then judge others unfairly as fools or liars when they adopt our words to describe us.

We know how frustrating it is when others treat us unfairly because of their biased assumptions; those presumptions occur often from seeing only a small portion of our behavioral spectrum. In turn, we do ourselves a similar injustice when inappropriately using limiting labels to describe ourselves. Rather than limit others and ourselves with negative or positive labeling, we should point out specific behaviors that are part of the types of actions we want to accomplish. We must encourage much more specific and descriptive language when we challenge ourselves or others to change. In this way, we can avoid pigeonholing either ourselves or others with stereotypic, blanket characterizations of behavior.

## TARGETS FOR CHANGE

Rather than assign general labels, it is better to describe troublesome aspects of a person's behavior in specific terms. Then, the specific behavior (arriving late at meetings, for example) becomes the target for change instead of an unfavorable generalized character trait that may have been unfairly attributed. With direct, constructive feedback and guidance, the employee stands a much better chance of arriving on time.

Even if we apply a label that accurately describes the person in a particular setting, it usually hinders the process of change. For example, "lazy" may narrowly apply to a person who has trouble getting reports in on time but is otherwise a hard worker. To be called lazy (or responded to as if the label were accurate) is destructive, as was mentioned earlier. Again, it is better to focus on specific behaviors that need to be changed. We should focus on what we actually see as opposed to what we merely hypothesize to exist.

If we give support to an employee for making small yet significant changes in behavior, those changes will become who he or she is. The employee can mature into a person who is focused on the task at hand, hardworking in the office, and sensitive to others' feelings. In time, the actions themselves take over and define the character or ethical values inferred from them, even if that employee chooses not to apply a label or continues to attach a negative label to these changes.

## PROCESSES OF BEHAVIOR CHANGE

We are now in a position to introduce readers to the actual processes involved in achieving ethical change. As we said at the beginning of the chapter, changing behavior of any kind, whether one's own or that of someone else, is not necessarily easy. It can be made *easier* if a foundation is laid in regard to the the way changes occur. Understanding the following processes increases an individual's and organization's effectiveness in implementing behavioral change procedures discussed in Chapter Eight.

The most effective procedures have been developed by behavioral psychologists. In what follows, we will outline four processes of change using the terminology of behavioral psychology: positive reinforcement, negative reinforcement, punishment, and extinction. Common ways of speaking about and defining these terms may seem at odds with the way these terms are used by psychologists. In our opinion, there is no substitute for the precision that these concepts introduce into a discussion of behavior change. However, the most important reason for introducing these concepts is that the methods work! When properly used, positive and negative reinforcement are immensely powerful tools. Punishing and extinguishing behavior can be extremely effective.

Positive reinforcement, negative reinforcement, punishment, and extinction are part of our everyday human interactions. We all use them to greater or lesser effect. The tools of science have counterparts in common experience. Unfortunately, these tools can be misused, used ineffectively, or used in ways that threaten personal autonomy or have other unethical consequences. We want to direct your attention to ways to use them with greater precision. In this chapter and the one that follows we describe *effective and ethical uses of behavior change processes.*

Both positive reinforcement and negative reinforcement increase the probability of a behavior occurring as a result of what the behavior produces. Punishment is the elimination or reduction of the occurrence of a behavior as a result of what the behavior produces. Extinction eliminates behavior, not through punishing it, but by withholding reward. It, too, is assessed in terms of whether or not a behavior stops.

Two of the processes obtain results through the threat of or the actual delivery of negative consequences. They are considered coercive: "...coercive control ... engenders side effects, often unintended, that poison our everyday social and institutional relationship."[1] Only one of the processes—positive reinforcement—is not coercive. "When we produce things or events that we ... consider useful, informative, or enjoyable for their own sake, we are under the control of positive consequences."[2]

Positive reinforcement is the only one of the processes where new behavior is produced as a direct consequence of a person's current actions. It increases the occurrence of behavior and makes it more likely that the person who is rewarded will continue to demonstrate actions that lead to rewards in the future. Not only will the behavior in question increase, but associated actions may as well.

Extinction, the fourth process, is not a process of reinforcement, nor is it directly coercive. Extinction can be used in a positive manner. For example, a manager may ignore an employee's problematic behaviors in a presentation—poor eye contact, rushed speech, failure to answer customer questions completely—and, instead, concentrate on the positive aspects of the presentation, rewarding instances of appropriate behavior that are in contrast with the errors. The manager might talk about good eye contact that she observed, the calm manner of presentation in the second half of the talk, or the direct and clear answer given to Mr. Jones—and indicate that more of these behaviors are what is needed to be even more effective. By ignoring the problematic behaviors, she is extinguishing them.

The example just discussed is an appropriate use of extinction. However, in most instances in the workplace, managers use extinction aversively, or negatively. It is this inappropriate use that we address here. A more complete analysis of the limitations and benefits of all these processes is available in psychology textbooks on learning.

Notice that all of these methods are defined in terms of their effect on behavior, not in terms of the intention of those who apply them. This is an important point. No matter what we want to do, if the behavior does not increase, we have not rewarded the person for it; positive reinforcement has not occurred. What is rewarding is defined by the person, not by those of us who want to change or increase an action through the use of what we define as rewarding. Similarly, if the behavior continues, we have not punished the person for it. Saying that reinforcers or punishers do not work really tells us more about our understanding of the terms and our skills in observing and dealing with behavior to get the actions we want. If we do not get the behavior we want, it is not rewards or punishers that fail. It is we who fail to correctly identify the necessary consequences required to produce the desired behavior.

The four processes are discussed in more detail below.

## Punishment

Punishment occurs when the immediate and direct use of words or actions stops behavior from recurring or decreases its frequency. Docking a person's pay can be punishing. So can firing someone. Saying "no" to a request or removing privileges, such as a company car, can be punishing. Whether or not any of these actually constitute punishment (in the technical sense in which we are using the word) depends upon the reaction of the individual being punished. Punishment, as technically defined, occurs only if the specific behavior in question diminishes or stops as a consequence of the action.

With punishment, incidental behavior can be as greatly or even more affected than the targeted behavior. For example, if the boss tells an employee she is stupid, the effect may not be any decrease in her "stupid" behavior, but only in the frequency of her approaches to the boss. The workplace situation will have been worsened, not improved.

In addition to the danger just alluded to, management strategies that focus too much on the use of aversive control are resented. Furthermore, aversive control demonstrates a lack of respect for autonomy. Unnecessary control over individual action usually results from a failure to understand how to increase independence. Individuals whose behavior is punished generally end up being more passive and taking fewer risks. Punishment often suppresses both the behavior intended and other, similar behaviors. Punishment becomes associated with the individual who uses it.

For punishment to be most effective, it must be immediate, but such immediacy means that the individual is under the review of someone else. Risking new ways of acting is discouraged in a system that relies on punitive control. Such control often requires the application of excessive rules and constant intervention and micromanagement of individuals. Such actions impede, if not defeat, the benefits that come with increased skill and autonomy.

## Negative Reinforcement

The second clearly coercive method of control is negative reinforcement. In contrast to punishment and extinction, negative reinforcement *increases* behavior, but it does so in an aversive fashion. Doing what is required in such cases means responding in order to remove or avoid an inhibiting or threatening action. Managers use this method with ease. "Do it or else" is described as a very common strategy for change used by managers. For example, the manager may say, "Unless you produce ten more widgets out of your crew by tomorrow morning, you will be moved back to your old position on the line." The reward for producing the ten widgets is to avoid returning to a lesser status and probably lower paying job— in other words, to escape from punishment. The manager's intended goal in using such a strategy is to increase productive behavior, but the conduct that also increases is avoiding interaction with the manager. The employee desires to escape or avoid the potential punishment.

The use of fear as a management strategy may produce results, but the effects are uncertain and the cost is high.

## Extinction

Extinction reduces and ultimately stops behavior. Extinction is the cessation of rewards for behavior. It eliminates or reduces the occurrence of a particular behavior or group of behaviors by the absence of a consequence, often by withholding attention or action. Managers often use extinction in the workplace when unwanted behavior occurs. An example is ignoring someone who talks too long during meetings and not calling on that person to speak. Over time, it is likely that the person will stop trying to talk. Because extinction is so easily available and sometimes unintentionally used, managers may apply this technique without understanding the powerful effect they are having on behaviors they desire to maintain. For example, managers may fail to acknowledge new ideas or suggestions from an employee. If attention from the manager is important to the individual, its absence will eliminate idea-generation over time.

Extinction is sometimes a benign process of withholding feedback to eliminate troublesome behavior. Extinction can, however, just as easily eliminate behavior that management views as desirable. While it is an easy method to use—if the manager can handle the process of ignoring a wildly waving hand or attempts to talk while the manager or others are talking—it is often slower than punishment or negative reinforcement strategies discussed above.

Extinction can have side effects. One of these may be a negative response to the person using the technique. For example, because being ignored may be embarrassing and unpleasant, an individual who feels that his or her behavior is being extinguished by another is less likely to seek out that person for any reason. The recipient's negative feelings may remain and have unwanted effects in the future.

## Positive Reinforcement

Positive reinforcement, like negative reinforcement, increases the occurrence of behavior. But it does so in a positive and not a negative way. When positively rewarded, people seek out the events and conditions that reward them. Examples of potential rewards include bonuses, kind words, time off, greater freedom, or better schedules. Just as with actions we assume to be punishing, these may or may not be rewarding depending upon what happens to the behavior in question. Kind words may not positively affect future behavior. Managers who use strategies that focus on examining and reinforcing appropriate action must be prepared to evaluate the effects—and interpret the data in terms of what is produced, not what is assumed should be produced.

Positive reinforcement requires an active process of observation and intervention that shapes the desired responses. When properly used, it leads to mastery of skills and effective performance.

Knowing whether or not we are reinforcing behavior requires perseverance, particularly when we are trying to develop new skills. This requires a willingness on our part, if we are managers, to change our supervisory style in a way that will let us take our cues for adjusting our responses from the actions produced. This commitment to using information about the effect of our actions in producing the response we want places the primary responsibility for change squarely on our shoulders as managers; we are responsible for the conditions we create in the workplace.

As indicated above, if we do not get behavior that is closer to what we want, it is not correct to say that "rewards" have failed. It means *we* have failed to correctly identify the contingent relation between behavior and what we need to do to change it. For example, a manager thanks an employee for making the extra effort to complete a job, but the employee does not find comments from that particular manager personally rewarding. The result may then be the opposite of what the manager wants. The employee may discontinue making extra efforts in order to avoid receiving praise from the manager. The behavior, extra effort in this case, has in effect been punished by the actions of the manager.

In order to apply this technique correctly, there is implied mutual accountability up and down the management ladder. The company and the manager must be evaluated on how well these conditions of management are applied. Careful, clear-eyed evaluation and flexibility of approach must be part of the expectation of the company. The company must set up conditions that ensure such management requirements are measured and evaluated. Managers must be under workplace contingencies that reinforce their effective use of positive reinforcement to improve performance.

Positive reinforcement can be misused, as can any of these processes. Companies can set up conditions that positively reinforce harmful actions—demeaning, threatening, or disinterested management, for example. Such companies in essence reward the managers for what they produce, ignoring how they get it done. That is why it is critical to tie business practices, including management styles, to a framework such as moral pluralism against which to evaluate the effects of "style" on employees. It is not sufficient just to evaluate business outcomes, no matter how successful.

## The Effects of Using Change Processes Coercively

Coercive methods to achieve change instill aversion and avoidance. Such methods generally take away the dignity of others, are often disrespectful, and diminish possible return on investment. In environments where coercion is used excessively, it is unlikely that individuals will speak out about new ideas, cost-saving ventures, innovative applications, or—what is most demoralizing—problems that exist.

There are times when the behavior of another is so self-de-
structive or destructive to others that coercive methods must be applied,
but this is rarely true. While such cases have been documented with
self-injuring autistic children, for example, the use of punishment at
work should be approached with much care. Punishment may have
to be used if an individual is actively threatening to others, commits
an illegal act, lies about a contract or other company commitment,
or does other outrageous and dangerous things. Such individual actions
need to be dealt with immediately through the use of effective ver-
bal punishment or withdrawal of other benefits. In some instances
the employee must be immediately dismissed.

In the vast majority of cases in which aversive control techniques are presently used in the business world, there is a better and
more ethical way to manage others. If this better way is applied across
the board, then punishment, negative reinforcement, and the inappropriate use of extinction are almost never needed.

Making personal or workplace ethical change offers the possibility of improving the everyday world in which we come in contact, as well as the world beyond our immediate sphere of influence.
We each have tremendous power to make a difference.

## NOTES

1.   Murray Sidman, *Coercion and Its Fallout* (Boston: Authors Cooperative, 1989), p. 37.
2.   Sidman, *Coercion*, p. 36.

# Designing Organizational Change

We envision a workplace where no one punishes, threatens, or cajoles anyone else. In such a workplace, managers do not manage, at least not in the usual sense. They do not worry about day-to-day problems in performance because the work atmosphere promotes the kinds of performance needed to create the best products and services. Managers and employees support one another in a positive and noncoercive manner to achieve the best for all, including the customer. Respect for the intrinsic worth and autonomy of everyone clearly is apparent.

We are describing a culture and a philosophy of action that says every individual, as part of the workplace, has the right to expect to be valued "as a rational creature, seeking reinforcement."[1] In such an environment, the corporate commitment is to find ways to reward people so as to maximize individual and group potential. It is a commitment to a moral society. It is achievable.

In Chapter Seven, we discussed the barriers to achieving ethical change and some of the processes by which behavior changes, including behaviors that define our ethical values. In this chapter, we examine methods for incorporating such change processes into the fabric of the workplace. We examine ways to design positively recurring consequences into daily practices to maintain and increase both profitability and an enlightened working environment. We discuss not only the process of change, but the need to structure consequences—incentives—so that change occurs in an ethical manner.

In the sort of workplace we are describing, each person examines the consequences of what he or she does to support colleagues

85

as they strive to do what is right, to achieve company objectives, and to generate profit. In such a setting, both managers and employees are accountable for evaluating the effects of their actions on each other and for behaving in ways that help everyone produce the best results. Policies, procedures, goal statements, planning documents, daily practice—all are colored by this reciprocal environment. Each employee has the potential to affect every other employee.

Unfortunately, few work settings are designed with this kind of human engineering in mind.

## MANAGEMENT SKILLS

A good place to begin this section is by examining differences between what management says and what it actually does in the workplace. For example, management might say that high quality is paramount. Yet high production is demanded and no inspection for errors is made; this sends a strong signal about what *really* counts. Saying that the company values teamwork while paying bonuses only to those who close the deals sends the same message. When employees are rewarded only for their own deal-making, it is unreasonable to expect them to put aside personal reward for the greater good of the team. They will respond to the contingencies of the workplace.

It is only if the relation between an action and its consequences is changed that we can expect behavior to change. Thus, if you as a manager want team behavior, you must determine not only how the individual can be rewarded for individual actions, but also how the group at the same time can be rewarded for total productivity. Under an ethical system, individuals and groups seek to promote the best from everyone, both internally and in relation to customers. Such a system must be particularly sensitive to the design of its incentives so that the commitment to customers promotes appropriate internal behavior. Having such a focus is part of the ideal workworld we envision.

Most managers have their jobs because they possess technical skills, not because they are skilled in the use of behavior change strategies. Many managers do not know how to change behavior by producing new, desirable ways of acting; instead they use techniques that get rid of undesirable behavior. Managers should be catching people doing the right thing, or approximations to the right thing, and rewarding them. Truly skillful managers of other people's behavior replace punishment with positive reinforcement whenever possible.

From the perspective of a busy manager, it may appear far more cost effective to deal with mistakes when they happen by punishing them rather than waiting to catch someone doing the right thing. Punishment can be swiftly carried out. Determining how to deliver punishment may seem simpler than the use of positively reinforcing techniques. The effects on those punished are clearly and usually immediately visible. Little time is required to see the results of the punishment.

In our opinion, managers much too frequently rely on coercive techniques: chewing people out when they make errors, writing them up when they miss a production quota, or publicly reprimanding them for stammering during a customer presentation. These techniques have validity on the surface. They seem to make the manager's job easier. Positive reinforcement, on the other hand, may seem less efficient.

We as managers may feel inclined to ask: Why not leave it up to individual employees to figure out how to bring about needed changes? After all, haven't we hired them because they know how to do what we want them to do? If things are not going as well as they should, why not leave it up to employees to figure out how to improve the situation? Otherwise, why pay them a salary in the first place?

But notice what we are doing: We are placing responsibility for change completely on the shoulders of the employee who is doing the wrong thing in the first place. We as managers are not accepting any responsibility for ourselves.

If we do accept responsibility, and we fail to produce desirable change in others through the management strategies we employ, we must try again using other strategies. We must find other methods that clearly express the unfavorable consequences of such behavior, hold responsible those who are explicitly accountable, and especially, measure results. When it becomes necessary, we must even change ourselves.

The manager's job in large part is to help the individual be the best that he or she can be. We can measure the supervisor's effectiveness by the effectiveness of the employees. It is equally important to recognize the ways that individual achievement is generally dependent upon the cooperation and actions of many, including the supervisor.

Even if managers are aware that the vast majority of workplace tasks require cooperation among many people, they may do little or nothing to systematically develop those relationships. Instead, they may give full credit to the one person who makes the sale, establishes the legal title, or develops a blueprint, usually ignoring the rest. Managers often think in terms of individual goal attainment. Changing this mind-set is one of the more important challenges facing American management practices today.

Take a thorough, dispassionate look at what is happening when we manage others. We are responding, just as employees do to us, to how the workplace rewards us. In turn, we respond to what our subordinates reinforce about us, although they rarely have sufficient power over the reinforcers of the workplace to make them as effective as might be desired in a truly reciprocal system. The reciprocal nature of what each of us does to the other and how such actions maintain or increase future actions cannot be minimized, especially where ethical change is involved.

## THE RESPONSIBILITY OF SENIOR MANAGEMENT

Even with all of the current books and seminars on management techniques, American business managers generally are not held accountable for *how* they achieve success, unless they do something totally outrageous. Instead, the measurement of a manager's effectiveness is based on goal attainment—profitability. Many aversive, threatening, unpleasant, and arrogant individuals are judged to be successful as managers because they satisfy or exceed predetermined goals for profits.

We say: If a manager achieves results using primarily aversive control techniques, that manager is cheating the company and employees. In turn, however, the company is cheating the manager by reinforcing him or her for using such techniques. In any case, where aversive techniques are used, important opportunities for new ideas, innovation, and risk taking may well be missed.

A company's chief opportunity is to use its employees to the fullest. If poor management strategies are accepted as they all too often are because profit is obtained, the company has failed to understand the consequences of such negative control strategies. It has failed to identify the potential gain that can occur through positive management techniques. It has cheated itself and its people.

As we have said before, success in business can be achieved at too high a price. If we as managers tell a subordinate, "I don't care how you do it—just get it done," we are treating business as amoral. What we do, regardless of what our more senior managers may say to us, will affect them, just as it immediately and directly affects our subordinates. There is synergy in the relationships. Understanding the nature of such reciprocal relationships is the key to creating optimal working conditions.

It is uncommon for managers to be held accountable by senior management not only for what needs to happen to satisfy profitability demands, but how noncoercively and ethically they produce the performance in others necessary to reach financial goals.

In addition, when employees fail to do their jobs, more of the responsibility for the failure belongs to management than to the individual employee. Why? Because the manager and the environment for which the manager is at least partly responsible have not provided what is necessary to get the results desired. Sometimes it is not possible to teach every individual, particularly those who lacked the needed skills to begin with, at a reasonable cost; even then, management bears responsibility for the results.

We advocate a management philosophy that says to employees: If you fail, we fail. If we succeed, you succeed. But if we fail, you may or may not have failed. If you succeed, we may or may not have succeeded. Regardless of what happens, we, the company, continue to bear responsibility for you the employee—to provide instruction and feedback, to observe your performance as carefully as we can and then respond in ways that are helpful to you while still supporting the company.

Is it fair to ask managers and those that manage them to be so concerned with all of these details and to carefully consider the effects their actions, or inactions, produce? Absolutely. Companies now waste inordinate amounts of time, energy, and resources in ill-conceived and rarely evaluated management strategies that all too often fail either to improve the workplace or to increase the likelihood of ethical actions.

## NATURAL CONSEQUENCES

Effective organizations creatively use naturally reinforcing systems that shape behavior unobtrusively and maintain it over time.

The systems themselves do the talking, as it were, while the worka-day exchanges between managers and subordinates focus on tasks and ideas concerning design, production, marketing, efficiency, safety, and other aspects of work life.

Well-designed workplaces are arranged to lead naturally to desired behaviors. Positive change is built into the fabric of the operation. Employees themselves become instruments of positive change. The energy of everyone, including managers, is redirected from concen-trating on problem performance to focusing on goal attainment and product/service enhancement.

An effective management system can be so positively reinforc-ing that there is no need for the threat of coercive action (escape, avoidance, or punishment) for noncompliance. Such a system sets up an environment from which positive reinforcers flow for positive actions, whether or not there is a specific individual present to praise performance. This type of work setting may include contingencies that support the pleasure of cooperative teams, the freedom to gen-erate and express ideas, the certainty that management actions and requests will be reasonable, and the responsibility to set one's own pace to effectively achieve specific goals.

Constructive policies and procedures that are "part of the fur-niture" are less intrusive while being more effective than rules that draw attention to themselves or positive benefits that are dependent solely upon individual action. The former are much less of a threat to autonomy; indeed they need not be a threat at all. As an analogy, the fact that a person will get wet in the rain without an umbrella is part of the "furniture of living" that plays a strong role in shaping people's behavior, yet no one feels threatened. Imagine how differ-ent it would be if prior to every rainstorm a voice in the clouds said: "Get out your umbrellas; we will punish those who do not do so by drenching them."

The rewards that a worker receives do not all come from management, nor does all of the punishment. Day in, day out, most workers are in contact with fellow employees, not managers. They are receiving feedback all the time from co-workers, and this feed-back can be rewarding or punishing. Establishing the expectation that individuals are evaluated on their own and others' effectiveness can lead to naturally occurring support for positive problem solving.

In Chapter Six, we discussed the value of making the work-place as pleasant as possible. The temperature of the workplace, the lighting, noise levels, and the comfort of furnishings all play a role in the workers' perception of whether or not management cares about them as human beings. Moreover, improvements in these matters belong to the "furniture of the system" that we mentioned earlier. A worker is not told: When you process ten more contracts per day, we will give you a more comfortable chair. Instead, the message is: We want your workday to be as productive *and* comfortable as possible. A new chair will help.

## DEMONSTRATING ETHICAL COMMITMENT IN THE WORKPLACE

Human beings seek environments that are rewarding and avoid those that are coercive. Allowing aversive control to dominate American management strategies is one way that we, as a society, are failing to harness the potential of the workplace. Too few work settings are designed to eliminate coercion.

Environments that rely too much on punishment and negative reinforcement suffer from the fallout that results from such negative control discussed in Chapter Seven. They are designed in such a way that concern and respect for others, the employees, even the customers, take a back seat to the notion that all is fair in generating profit. This is neither true nor ethical.

Managers sometimes believe incorrectly that to praise is to belittle achievement. "I hired them to do the job and, by damn, they better do the best job they can if they expect to be here next year. I don't give them M&Ms for just doing their jobs. And I do get results. You can't argue with results."

To that we say, nonsense! There are better ways to achieve results—better both ethically and as sound management practice. Any senior executive who knows about the aversive styles of his or her managers and does nothing to change those actions fails to address the real issues.

There are numerous barriers that stand in the way of optimal business success. Divisions between units, unnecessary competition, unfair practices, and misunderstanding are some of the critical elements that may preclude optimal performance. If there are structural barriers that keep one unit from talking to another or one individual from combining talents with another individual, these barriers

are serious impediments to the widest opportunity to comment about
activity, and to ensure candid review, including the ethics of particular actions.

The employees need to know that the best combination is what
is expected. They should not be driven by a system of formal per-
mission but rather by incentives to "get the job done in the best way
possible."

Focus on the dissemination of information; describe plans for
the company's operations and how the employee's efforts fit in. Invite
debate and ask for suggestions for change. Implement such change
where it is possible and practical.

## ENDURING COMMITMENT TO AN ETHICALLY
## DESIGNED WORKPLACE

While each manager is crucial to the effective application of
positive processes of change, the overall picture is more enduring if
the organization creates "top down" strategies of change. The company must establish its workplace as a mutually reinforcing environment for all individuals who enter it, including senior executives,
managers, and employees. The reciprocal nature of using positive
reinforcement is fundamental to its capacity to rapidly increase the
likelihood of positive and supportive actions. "As I set up conditions for you to change, and you change, I then change. As we change,
the company changes. As you are rewarded, I am rewarded. As we
create positive outcomes, the customer benefits and the company is
rewarded."

In such a setting, the manager's behavior is shaped not only
from above, but also by the positive responses of subordinates. The
senior executive is shaped by the behavior of subordinates. The latter
will be encouraged to respond in a helpful and positive way when
the ethical commitment of the company is visible to everyone. Specific behavioral objectives to measure the ethical sensitivities of the
workplace should be built into each individual and group performance appraisal, as well as company-wide planning documents. Every
evaluation of the company's effectiveness must consider both profit
and loss statements and how well the company has achieved ethical
objectives.

The goal is to use positive and reciprocal management strategies measured against the principles of moral pluralism to generate
optimal and ethical performance from everyone.

## NUTS AND BOLTS: STEPS NEEDED TO
## PRODUCE REAL CHANGE

The steps outlined in this section apply equally to organizations and individuals. Most people can begin the process of change by following the steps outlined below. However, there are no instant remedies. Maintaining ethical change requires persistent and behaviorally sophisticated efforts across the organization.

*1. Identify the ethical change required.*

Before we can bring about change, we must first identify what needs to be changed. As we said in Chapter Seven, when identifying the targets for change, we must focus on specific behaviors that are problematic, not general labels. Not: "We must get Sam to be more reliable." Instead: "We must get Sam to turn in sales reports promptly." Not: "Mary is disrespectful." Instead: "Mary frequently interrupts others in a loud voice." Not: "Ed is not committed to the good of the group." Instead: "Ed does not express his opinions during planning sessions."

Before you can embark on producing behavior changes, you will have to ask clarifying questions about what precisely is wanted, especially when a desirable ethical outcome is the aim. Look to current actions and their consequences. Ask yourself what, for example, maintains the current behavior you do not want or reduces behavior you want to increase in frequency.

*2. Outline the specific steps required to achieve the targeted outcome.*

Describe where you want to go (the destination or outcome to be achieved) and outline how you want to get there (the steps to be taken). Use a process similar to goal setting where objectives, steps to achieve results, by whom and when, and methods of evaluation are identified. This component of personal or organizational change is sometimes fuzzy, often left to our good "intentions" rather than described in observable and measurable terms.

It is often helpful to first analyze the conditions for change in general terms, then progress to examining specific issues. For instance, one person contributes to a meeting by offering opinions and speaking eloquently. Another person may talk just as eloquently to a colleague "off the record" while exiting the conference room; he has the general skills but does not apply them in the setting required.

It is not an "ethical" shortcoming when one does not speak in a team meeting. However, it takes on ethical significance when one who has something to say keeps quiet during discussions that have moral consequences regarding rights, justice, the common good, or self-interest; that can become a problem for you, as well as diminish the effectiveness of the group. In the specific instance of teams, we each rely on the other to point us in the right direction and support us. Giving one's best advice *is* an ethical obligation in such situations. Learning how to do so as a matter of course, with good humor and sincerity, involves skills that require a hospitable environment and successive support for steps in the right direction.

Once such observational information has been collected, you will have a good indication of which behaviors need to be increased. These should be broken down into specific steps, as concretely as possible. It is not possible, in most situations, to identify every aspect of the needed changes, nor is it usually necessary.

*3. Use every avenue available to establish conditions to promote ethical change.*

If you are a manager, you have a number of different options available to reach your objectives: building group understanding through team meetings; examining company policies and procedures that support the actions you want; conducting regular performance appraisal sessions to allow both you and others a way to evaluate change.

If your goal is ethical behavior change for yourself as an employee, you often have to rely more on yourself to make such changes. Still, others can help, including your manager. Tell your manager what you want to do. It may be that you want to demonstrate more respect for others by improving your listening and communication skills. Your manager can help you introduce effective strategies into daily practice and can help in the evaluation of change. Also, fellow employees can be asked to support your efforts.

In addition, there may be company policies or procedures that provide an orderly way to bring to the attention of senior management recommended changes that could improve the ethical atmosphere of the company. Depending on your position in the organization and the resources available to you, you might:

• Characterize the nature of the ethical issues, the areas you interact

with directly, and how you might structure your plan of action to address meaningful aspects within your areas of influence.
- Inform others of your goals.
- Ask for their advice about both your and the organization's actions and how most constructively to increase overall sensitivity to the ethical implications of actions.
- Hold meetings in which "case studies" or other methods are used to increase for all employees, including yourself, ethical sensitivity to issues. Use the comments to evaluate the level of awareness and to refine current steps and better define needed next steps.
- Build into the performance review system an assessment of the ethical conduct of employees in achieving objectives. Make sure, if you are a manager, that your manager holds you accountable in the same manner.
- Require an "ethical analysis" in any planning documents at the unit, department, office or company level, and establish clear review dates and procedures.

Be clear about what details are required to move you further toward your goal. Examine barriers that get in the way, such as the following excuses: "I have other responsibilities"; "I am too busy"; "I must look after new customers."

## 4. Practice the new behaviors.

After you have pinpointed the target for change, identified what was maintaining or keeping the needed actions from occurring, outlined the steps needed to remove barriers and reinforce new performance, you must then set up conditions that produce the newly defined, desired behaviors.

The example above about speaking out in meetings on ethical issues provides a useful framework for establishing the organizational conditions to evoke the new behaviors. Learning to talk about important matters, especially in a group setting, can be difficult. First, announce your goal. If you are doing this as part of a system-wide change strategy, then the commitment to open discussion must be publicly stated to all employees, comments must be sought, and when small increases in the occurrence of such comments are made by people who generally may not make such statements, the manager must actively encourage (and hopefully reinforce) them. At the organizational level, the incentives for producing and increasing the desired behaviors rest, not with the individual, but with the conditions of the workplace.

The manager must understand that he is evaluated on how well he increases employee's positive, constructive talk about significant business issues of an ethical nature. The manager's job is to ensure that candid as well as appropriate expression is perceived as the norm.

If you are making such changes by yourself, set up the conditions by first telling trusted others what you want to do and how you want them to respond to you. Small steps can be practiced first; for example, before speaking up wholly on your own, you could speak in support of a statement made by another member of the discussion group, or reword the statement to be sure it is understood. This practice will help prepare you to confront and expound upon controversial issues in various settings.

You may need to actually go into the conference room alone and practice such statements out loud, to increase your level of comfort in that setting, which may remind you of a setting where you were inhibited from expressing yourself. Such associations in the environment are often ignored, but previous experience can be recalled all too easily when walking into the environments where such actions occurred.

A suggestion: Take a trusted friend into the aversive setting. Have that friend listen to you in that setting. Sometimes, the new association—being with someone you like in an unpleasant setting—can help in reducing aversion.

### 5.  Invite feedback and instruction.

When we undertake change, it is important that we have someone to oversee the new actions closely and provide feedback and analysis for the developing changes. This person can make positive comments and, when necessary, tactfully suggest a mid-course correction.

A company that really wants to improve its ethical sensitivities needs to expect that such change is difficult to implement, particularly if managers have become accustomed to other strategies that up to this point have always worked. Organizations need to avoid having the "blind leading the blind." Sometimes it is worthwhile to have an outside observer provide comment. Sometimes peer managers or someone from a different area of the operation may recognize what is needed and be good at defining its presence or absence in others. These are the people who may make the best coaches. Remember, changes in style are unlikely unless the contingencies applied actively reinforce the right actions.

Managers can, as well, seek the evaluative critique of their employees. They can ask directly for comments about what they need to do to promote a more open environment. They can also make meetings open to evaluation. At the end of an representative meeting, a survey of two or three questions can be distributed, asking the group to describe what worked and what did not. Such a system does not require that everyone in the meeting "get their way," nor does allowing employees to evaluate the boss undermine the boss's effectiveness. In fact, if correctly designed, this system can provide appropriate feedback to the manager and demonstrate the reciprocal nature of the company's genuine commitment.

You might want to select a colleague who will support your efforts during the meeting and help you assess your actions afterward. These steps may seem unnecessary, but there is no better way to change expectations and promote behavior change than to actively involve others in the plan. Such public commitment puts in motion another contingency to help us persist—other people's expectations. Positive feedback and constructive criticism that offer alternatives can reinforce our ability to change actions or attitudes of ourselves and others.

Placing the evaluation of our effectiveness in the hands of others is threatening. Supportive commitment, treating managers as well as employees with respect, assuming they are trying to do the right thing, is important to such a process. Both giving and getting feedback in such a system must be designed to be constructive and focused on solutions.

### 6. "Reward yourself."

Tell others when changes occur. If a department or an office or an individual helps you achieve a change that you have been working toward, thank them. Positive feedback is a two-way street. Others are more likely to consistently treat you as a person who has truly changed when you tell them about your success and your determination to continue to behave differently. They are more likely to make positive comments without prompting. They become part of the natural consequences that help you maintain change.

When you are in the role of providing support for other people's change, be generous, genuine, and specific in your praise and/or criticism. Evaluate what you say according to what actually happens. This point cannot be emphasized enough. It is not in what we want to have happen, but rather in what does happen that we best define the kinds of actions we take in supporting change. In whatever aspect of the change process you find yourself, never assume that there are "rules" about how you are to act. You must observe, intervene or not intervene, and observe once again. Do whatever it takes to help your colleague(s) reach the goal; that includes praising or constructively criticizing their effort and providing clear direction as needed. It also may include supporting the change through your own actions—such as by speaking yourself in support of someone who has just spoken at a meeting.

What we tell ourselves privately can either reinforce and strengthen or punish and decrease significant actions. For targeted behaviors, we must chart our own progress and reward ourselves through an internal system of private assessment—what we tell ourselves through our thoughts—or through the use of notes or actual graphs to record improvement. We must be fair and honest with ourselves, without being overly negative, when assessing our own actions. An example would be to say: "I really tried and I was able to tell the boss that I supported Joe's argument during the meeting. Next time I'll do better and make an independent comment."

*7. Evaluate the effects of ethical change.*

If you achieve the outcome you want, consider your plan for change a success, at least in the short run. If your plan does not work, then identify the point at which it failed. Begin working again from that point. Regardless, the change must become part of the daily activity, part of what is supported in the environment.

## NOTE

1.   Richard Garret, "Practical Reason and a Science of Morals," in *B. F. Skinner: Consensus and Controversy*, eds. Sohan Modgil and Celia Modgil (New York: Falmer Press, 1987), p. 327.

# CHAPTER NINE

# Workplace Ethics and the Quality Imperative

A revolution in management practices is overtaking American businesses, primarily in response to competitive pressures from abroad during the last decade. W. Edwards Deming and J. M. Juran are sometimes spoken of as the founding fathers of this revolution, which is often called the "quality movement" or the "quality imperative." Its major tenets and principles have been extensively discussed and are summarized as follows:

- Do not blame poor-quality products and services on individual employees. In most cases, the fault lies with systems of management.
- Design business systems where every detail is oriented toward satisfying customers. This advice applies to "external customers" who buy products and services from the business and equally to "internal customers" in the next office who work for the same company.
- To achieve success, cooperate. Coordination between producers and suppliers, employers and employees, designers and manufacturers, is essential.
- To save money in the long run, design high-quality products and services that best serve customers.
- Supplement short-term goals ("management by objectives") with greater reliance on long-term goals.
- Push decision-making down into the ranks from top levels of management. Eliminate middle management layers wherever possible.

- Replace motivation based on fear with motivation based on pride in a job well done.
- "Empower" people to do their best—by encouraging them to take the initiative and by removing barriers to their productivity and problem-solving abilities.
- Minimize the possibility of human error through the improved design of all workplace procedures and systems; these include manufacturing, delivery within the company and to clients, and informational systems. For example, design parts so that they cannot possibly be assembled in the wrong way.
- Guard against the "domino effect" in product design and use— a fault in one area should not cause problems elsewhere. For example, choose a noncorrosive material that can withstand chemical leaks from adjacent components of a machine.
- Reduce pollution and improve health and safety for workers and consumers.
- Make workers' jobs more meaningful, and morale and productivity will improve.

The overall direction of the quality movement supports an ethical perspective. Making work more meaningful, increasing cooperation in the workplace, enhancing autonomy, improving conditions for health and safety, and making the workplace more participatory are all goals of the quality movement that are laudable from a moral perspective. It is not far from the truth to say that the basic maxim of the quality movement is:

> Treat everyone well—customers, employees,
> fellow workers, suppliers, etc.

There are, however, some dark clouds on the horizon as American businesses move to adapt themselves to the new styles of management.

## "TOTAL COMMITMENT"

The quality imperative states that employees must be integral parts of the companies they work for, both in how they function within the system and in terms of their attitudes and commitments. Employees who more fully understand the company as a whole can help solve its problems and contribute to its long-term success. For its part, the company must tap all of the problem-solving capacities that its employees possess. Quality-driven companies make maximum use of their employees' talents, energy, and dedication. As much as possible, these businesses enhance the employees' sense of "belonging to the company."

The danger is that the individual will be swallowed up by the corporation.

> What these "work hard, play hard" companies want is nothing less than total responsibility and over-the-edge loyalty. . . ."[1]

A person's individuality can be lost in an organization that requires an excessive degree of loyalty and commitment. In striving to elicit the absolute best from every employee, managers may demand too much. And it is not just managers who may do this; employees may demand too much of one another and of themselves. From a moral perspective, it is essential that businesses adopting "quality management" remember that employees have their own lives apart from the company.

Allow employees their hobbies, political interests, leisure time, and family life. In an atmosphere designed to elicit new ideas, allow employees to express differences of opinion about office procedures and corporate goals, particularly those diverging from company perspectives. It is equally essential that managers help individual employees recognize the need to take time for themselves. In turn, managers need to be alert to their own needs in this regard. Deming has said: "We have to restore the individual."[2]

Ethical behavior in the workplace requires finding a balance among potentially conflicting values: work versus family, need for leisure time versus the need to complete job assignments promptly, loyalty to the company versus commitment to social causes that may conflict with corporate goals. There are many other conflicts. Respect for individuality requires not glossing over or ignoring them.

Even in companies dedicated to the quality imperative, it is difficult for individual employees to risk displeasing the boss, especially in the realm of ideas or for the sake of commitments to family and outside life. Managers must be sure that they give recognition to the personal lives and perspectives of employees apart from the corporation. This will happen only when the executive leadership understands the need for it and requires that managers be evaluated in terms of criteria such as "openness to employee ideas" and "commitment to the individuality of employees." These criteria can be specified in behavioral terms and measured.

In many instances, managers will need to acquire new skills to enable them to respond to innovative ideas from employees and to employees' requests for time with families. "Total quality management" requires that managers implement workplace changes in response to employee openness and individuality. Managers usually have the greatest control in this area.

In "old style" authoritarian companies a large gap exists between the company and the lives of its employees. The company management seldom discusses with employees goals and plans that might affect their lives. This omission sends a strong, negative, damaging message to employees. However, in "new style" companies of the future, the pendulum may swing too far in the opposite direction if there is not enough of a clear delineation between private life and company life.

The achievement of balance and respect for individual autonomy become all the more important as both workers and employers embrace the ideas involved in making employees "partners" within the workplace. In the midst of creating new levels of energy, commitment, and enthusiasm in the workplace, the quality imperative may also create blind spots in regard to the employee's need for personal time.

## STRETCH GOALS

The "commitment to quality" puts pressure on everyone in the workplace to achieve perfection. Consider this "new style" manager's comment:

> In the early 1980s about 92 per cent of the parts coming into our Webster, New York plant were defect-free. From a competitive standpoint that is absolutely abominable. We're now at 99.95 per cent, which is absolutely unsatisfactory. . . . We believe 100 per cent defect-free is possible, and that is our expectation now. . . .[3]

It is possible for products to be 100 percent defect-free; such an expectation can be reasonable and realistic. But in striving for perfection, managers face another difficult area where balance needs to be achieved. At what cost to worker morale does a company move from 99.95 percent to 100 percent? When workplace expectations are set too high, they can both exhaust and demoralize individuals.

Workplaces committed to the quality imperative frequently set "stretch goals"; these are goals that exceed prior achievements. They can be extremely effective motivators. Fulfilling them can be highly rewarding. If given the opportunity, employees may set even greater goals for themselves than their managers have set. Stretch goals can also be damaging.

What conditions might lead to unreasonable expectations in the workplace? The following are prime examples: timeframes that are unrealistic; tasks that are assigned unfairly and inappropriately in relation to skills, knowledge, and the abilities of particular workers; production standards that are shifted arbitrarily. Here and elsewhere, a point is reached beyond which expectations are destructive or at least excessively stressful.

From the perspective of profit-making, unreasonable expectations are likely to backfire. Unreasonable demands produce a variety of negative reactions, including resentment, anxiety, and fatigue. Our view is that even if setting unreasonably high expectations were the most profitable strategy, doing so would be unethical. We have said it before: *Success in business can be achieved at too high a price.*

Sometimes enthusiastic managers say: "We set high standards around here. Anything less than 100 percent is not acceptable—100 percent in terms both of your effort and your output." Such hyperbole is common and most employees understand that it is not meant literally, but rather as inspiration. Such talk can reflect endorsement and enthusiasm for the hard work of everyone. We expect a football team in a national championship to do its absolute, literal best. But under normal conditions of life, expecting the absolute best from oneself or one's employees can place an intolerable burden upon the individual. Virtually no one can maintain his or her best for any length of time.

Words can create their own reality. When hearing the manager's high expectation, employees may think in terms of "perfect performance." They may move beyond what was originally said and add their own unreasonable requirements to such things as production rates and service calls. Employees who fail under such conditions often feel inadequate or guilty. New management in the 1990s requires the most careful review of expectations and outcomes.

## BANISHING FEAR FROM THE WORKPLACE

The establishment of unreasonably high expectations is a more sophisticated version of the old authoritarian style of managing. In the old style, a boss said: "We tolerate no more than five defective products per 1,000." It did not matter what the real causes of the defects were, whether they were under the control of the individual employee or not. He or she was simply told, "No more than five defects, period." How was this 99.5 percent level to be achieved? Somehow. If it was not achieved, then the threat of recriminations was constantly present. Employees worked in perpetual fear.

Fear about job performance and security exists today whether employees operate under old or new styles of management. Individuals know that failure to achieve company objectives threatens their jobs. The manager must establish realistic goals and use noncoercive styles of management if fear is to be removed from the workplace. Elimination of fear requires that employees fully understand the conditions of their employment and that those conditions be predicated upon fair practices. Management must carefully and clearly define corporate goals and help employees understand what they are required to do to achieve those goals. Changes in strategy or operational focus require explanation as well if the company's actions are not to appear arbitrary and capricious.

When management violates the requirement for providing a psychologically safe work setting, they are not complying with Deming's admonition: Managing by fear must be banished.

Business people who believe in the superiority of free market exchange sometimes fail to see that they have created within their own companies an authoritarian organization where individual employees are subject to heavy-handed control. A free market orientation has as much relevance to processes within a corporation as to processes external to it. A free market does not have heavy-handed directives imposed upon it from outside. Its direction arises from within, more spontaneously, more in concert with individual autonomy than happens in a controlled economy. This same idea has application on a smaller scale within corporations; it has, in fact, become a part of the "quality revolution," which is committed to autonomy and is radically opposed to authoritarian styles of management.

A good manager who is committed to the quality imperative expects that each employee wants to do a good job and can improve. The manager is equally committed to the idea that the employee can help the manager to improve his or her performance as well. The manager, the contingencies established in the workplace, and the employees all together help to bring about improvement in performance and in the conditions for work. When problems arise in individual performance, the manager determines whether goals are clearly understood and if the skills and knowledge of the worker need to be improved; the manager is quick to praise or redirect behavior.

In such a system, managers do not create dependency on themselves, but create environments that invite problem-solving efforts. They actively seek solutions whether inside or outside their areas of responsibility. The "new manager" understands how to build positive performance from subordinates and maintain it, and how to work with peers to bring about change.

## LOYALTY TO THE COMPANY

Rewarding employees for "supreme loyalty" to the company is a frequent but dangerous practice. All too often loyalty is perceived as the unstated but clearly understood reason for promoting a person whose chief talent lies in saying "yes" to the boss. It is a reason sometimes not to address performance problems. There are dedicated employees who are both highly productive and loyal in the sense of demonstrating a positive attitude and providing extra effort when it is needed. Reward this kind of loyalty.

The important question is not how "loyal" an employee is, but rather: In what ways do an employee's actions further the objectives of the company? All too often, managers encounter poorly performing individuals who are "loyal" beyond measure. Companies often reward these people for their unquestioning obedience, in spite of poor performance in other areas. What such an approach does is to reduce dissension and increase cynicism. Until loyalty is specified in behavioral terms and is measured by its effects, it has little intrinsic value and leaves much room for misunderstanding.

All too often, employees are afraid that they will be perceived as disloyal. Management must examine closely how the corporate culture is structured. Are employees allowed to speak out on such matters as the defense of unpopular positions? Are they reinforced for taking risks and bringing to the attention of other employees, and also supervisors, decisions that are not good for the company? Management must reinforce assertiveness that benefits the company.

Supreme, total loyalty has no place in the "new management" philosophy. Rewarding it while ignoring other aspects of performance violates autonomy and produces resentment. It is another form of coercion.

## MANAGEMENT BY NUMBERS

Managing by numbers alone—volumes, rates, dollars, frequencies, percentages of a goal—is well understood by workers. But it is not adequate to create a culture committed to either ethical behavior or high-quality goods and services. Deming and others who speak for the quality movement reject numerical goals as the sole criterion for running a business. While quotas and other numerical goals are often used as measurement tools and do serve a practical function, when they are treated as the sole criterion for achievement, they are misleading and limit achievement. Suppose, for example, that an electronics firm sets a goal of 40 television sets to be produced per day. It is likely that the firm will get 40 units per day, but the sets may not last through the warranty period. Similarly, a company that requires each salesperson to make 100 sales calls per month may get the numbers, but they tell us nothing about the substance of the calls. Producing high-quality goods and services requires a careful examination of multiple dimensions involved, such as volume, preparation time, rate, and standards against which to measure outcome. Management must define individual performance objectives in relation to such dimensions. Measurement that focuses on a single dimension is not adequate. Assuming that individuals can achieve quality objectives without specifying these and other criteria for achieving excellence is unrealistic.

## FAIRNESS TO WOMEN AND MINORITIES

Another area that requires sensitive management is the area of gender and minority diversity. We all feel demeaned when we receive stereotypical treatment as members of a group rather than as unique individuals with our own special talents and interests. Women often face obstacles in the workplace that are brought upon them not by their performance, but by their gender and how others perceive them. Minority group members have problems based on the biases and perceptions of others. Once again, performance is not the issue—unfairly, their minority situation is the issue. A sensitive manager must be aware of such problems.

Members of minority or disadvantaged groups may be reluctant to take full advantage of structures that support advancement, particularly in systems dominated by the majority. For example: The personnel department has hired a woman as a technical assistant in an engineering department composed only of male engineers. She shows an aptitude for her job but waits for someone to point out that she would do well as an engineer. Not only may she be less likely to ask for support to take engineering courses in order to advance herself, but others may be less likely to think of her in terms of advancement and self-improvement than they would of a man in the same job position. A good manager will not ignore this differential, but will provide additional encouragement and actively support the woman's efforts at self-improvement and advancement. Most of us, male or female, respond to what others expect of us to some extent. Active encouragement about our potential to achieve is one way to open a new door.

Similarly, a good manager is alert to problems of communication, whether written or oral. Such problems may affect minorities whose primary language is not English or who have insufficient training in the proper use of English. A good manager will not ignore such difficulties or allow them to get worse, but will offer whatever help is available to improve necessary skills. A manager serves the employee poorly when that employee continues to make errors of speech or written communication; the manager's desire to not offend the employee is no excuse, as ultimately both the employee *and* the company lose out.

Although under ideal conditions gender and minority membership should be disregarded, we are not advocating a "gender-blind" or "color-blind" management policy; such a policy is one where a manager purposefully ignores problems associated with distinctions between men and women, majorities and minorities. Such a manager might say: "All people are treated equally here." In reality, "equality" in the workplace does not exist. The treatment that people in fact receive is dependent upon membership or perceived membership in various groups. Sensitive management must strive to understand and respond ethically to both the advantages and the disadvantages of group membership.

## SHARING INFORMATION

For "new management" styles to be successful, managers must inform their employees of the company's goals, precisely of the specific corporate intent. Product design, markets, systems for delivering services, performance expectations, make up one part of corporate direction. Another is the broad "corporate philosophy," the company's strategic goals and its value system. If employees are kept in the dark about significant company policies and viewed simply as cogs on the company wheel, they will not be able to contribute as bona fide team members.

Managers of American companies have frequently worried that an open information dissemination policy of this sort would let company "secrets" leak to competitors. Certainly that danger exists, but we believe that the benefits of openness outweigh the risks. We believe that it is better to deal with the question of disclosure on a moral level through a company code of ethics that spells out the need for confidentiality and discretion, rather than running a company as a miniature police state.

## TRAINING

Closely tied to a policy of openness is the emphasis upon training that is an essential part of the quality revolution. Most management structures have supported training in some form, on the sound belief that workers will do a better job if the company trains them effectively. Going beyond that, the new emphasis from the quality movement is on the worth of the individual as a major contributor to the corporation. One of the principles of the quality movement is to treat employees well. The 1990s are a time of increased worker selectivity; workers may decide to change jobs even after the investment in their training. Nevertheless, a company's investment may make it less likely that employees will leave. If management trains employees to do more than a single job, the "cross-trained" employees will provide much more help when it is needed in other areas. They better understand the impact of their actions on one another and are more likely to be seen as integral parts of the larger company.

Moreover, cross-training provides employees with greater information about the company as a whole. It gives them hands-on information, the kind that cannot be put into instruction booklets. Such training provides a cushion in case a particular department or division is scaled back or closed down. Employees are already trained for other positions.

In addition to considering how more extensive training benefits the company directly, managers have a further ethical responsibility to their employees when it comes to training. It is not enough for an employee to "know" that training is available. The new styles of management place emphasis on the role of the manager "in service" to employees.[4] This means that it is incumbent upon the manager to evaluate performance and to find ways to help employees succeed. Passive responses—"it's her fault if she does not succeed here or does not take advantage of training"—are no longer acceptable. The manager assumes a responsibility to arrange the workplace so it provides an atmosphere that allows employees to develop fully and thus contribute more to the organization.

## LESSENING INTERNAL COMPETITION

Actual head-to-head competition within an organization can be quite destructive. It can be reduced by adopting management policies that assign value to individuals in concert with others—well before they have competitively produced a new product design, a new sales plan, or a new investment strategy. For example, rather than have management tell three people to each produce a complete sales plan from which the "best" will be chosen while the other two will be discarded, another strategy is to tell all three that they will be asked to develop a plan together. One of the three might be asked to produce a draft plan to save time. The other two employees are left free to work elsewhere. Then a brainstorming session is conducted among the three to determine how to improve the initial plan. This method potentially can provide some recognition to the one person who is asked to write the draft, while placing the real emphasis on collective activity to produce an outcome. The lessening of competition comes when the contingency is placed, not on the individual creating a plan with the "help" of colleagues, but rather, on the collective creation of a plan. Cooperation increases when incentives are designed that require teamwork. All too often the workplace uses incentives to produce competitive, individualistic action.

Excessive competition hinders team efforts. Walls are built

between units of a company that could do a better job if they shared their knowledge. It is better to reduce competition among employees within departments of the same company, and to reduce competition between departments and divisions. The incentives that generate competition must be carefully evaluated as to their real effect on behavior. Competition can easily be a most destructive part of the work environment.

This is not to say that there should be no competition at all within a company, but competition divides individuals if used internally as a strategy to motivate people. Much more is gained when competition is designed either as an external target or as something individuals impose themselves to measure their own performance. The focus of the company should be on breaking down barriers and increasing cooperative action to the greatest extent possible.

## EMPLOYERS AND FAMILIES

In most American families today both spouses work. The responsibility for raising children (in some cases supporting elderly parents at the same time) frequently requires two incomes. Good day care for children is needed. Sometimes elder care is also needed. In the years to come, the work force will shrink as members of the baby boom generation come to retire. The need for skilled employees will then increase. Companies must also consider replacement costs for women who leave the work force because they cannot find acceptable care for children. The business world can no longer afford to ignore the needs of contemporary families.

Only now, in the 1990s, are companies beginning to develop plans for both daily child care and other family-related concerns of employees. Some of these companies are described in a recent book, *Companies That Care*.[5] If employees are to become true team members of the organizations they work for, then corporations must become members of the other "team" to which employees belong, namely, their families.

## AUTOMATION

A further area where today's corporations need to adjust humanely to changing times concerns factory and office automation.

It is clear that many of today's jobs will not exist tomorrow, replaced by improvements in automation. The decisions about when, how, and where to automate are particularly difficult for corporate leaders. Saving money and maintaining a competitive edge sometimes make automation the only responsible choice. Jobs may be lost; many jobs will be transformed.

Automation can be humanized through sensitive planning, giving fair warning, exercising care in examining options where employees might transfer, and creating well-structured phase-out programs. When automation does not eliminate jobs, it often changes existing jobs or creates wholly new jobs. In a company committed to training, such changes will be more likely viewed as opportunities rather than threats.

## INNOVATION AND JOB SECURITY

No one in the work force wants to suggest a labor-saving innovation for the company if the labor saved means the elimination of that person's job. By contrast, employees who feel secure in a company because of its employment history and clear policies and who are broadly trained for work in various areas of the company are a most valuable asset. They feel themselves genuinely to be part of a team effort. They are likely to enjoy solving work problems. They welcome increased automation and innovation.

Every company should guarantee absolutely that no one in the organization will be eliminated from employment as a result of suggesting a more efficient way to get the job done—even if the suggestion demonstrates that the person's job is totally unnecessary.

Even aside from the question of establishing workplace conditions that will encourage employees to come forth with new ideas, employees should be given as much security in their jobs as possible. Job security cannot be absolutely guaranteed in corporations that must remain competitive, but, once again, there must be an effort to establish clear policies that avoid capricious actions against employees.

Security is one of the most important values in life, directly tied to happiness for most people. One requirement for job security is knowing what is required for success in the job. Further, a secure employee expects fair treatment, that credit will be given for effort made, and that the company will honor all its commitments. Such security increases the likelihood that employees will invest in their companies, giving their best advice and guidance, and approaching the workplace with energy.

## INDUSTRY-WIDE STANDARDS

The last topic we will cover in this chapter is the creation of voluntary industry-wide standards. There are two kinds, both of them necessary to support ethical decision-making and the quality imperative.

First, ethical standards can be embodied in codes of conduct that are developed industry-wide for all companies that sell similar products or services. The standards are strengthened when formulated and accepted by all the companies that normally compete against each other in a segment of the market. Such standards provide a road map for the customer and are a help to companies in designing their products and services. Another reason for developing codes industry-wide is that no company by itself will bear any additional expenses that may be incurred when the standards are upheld, and individual companies are given a certain measure of protection in times of dispute or litigation. Managers can say: We did adhere to ethical standards recognized by the entire industry. We were doing our best at the time, acting in good faith.

Acting in good faith will be strengthened if each company evaluates its own standards against those that apply industry-wide. If the industry-wide code is incomplete or vague, then the company's own code can make up for these deficiencies.

The second kind of standard is for the performance of products. Such standards range from standardization of thread types and sizes for screws and bolts to target figures for miles per gallon in cars, quality standards for materials, underwriting requirements, accounting practices, safety standards for operating machines, etc. Again, companies are given a measure of protection when disputes arise, but more important, customers are likely to receive better products and services at lower prices. Standardization reduces error and the potential for cutting corners. It increases efficiency, effectiveness, and safety. It may increase costs initially, but over time should reduce labor, materials, and replacement costs.

A key to the process of negotiating standards across industry groups is finding common interests to rally around while promoting cooperative goodwill that transcends company boundaries. The establishment of many more industry-wide standards is another of the broad goals of the quality revolution. We will return to the topic of industry-wide standards in the next chapter.

## NOTES

1. David Kirp and Douglas Rice as quoted in Joseph H. Boyett and Henry P. Conn, *Workplace 2000: The Revolution Reshaping American Business* (New York: Dutton, 1991), p. 40.

2. W. Edwards Deming as quoted in Rafael Aguayo, *Dr. Deming: The American Who Taught the Japanese About Quality* (New York: Fireside, 1990), p. 122.

3. David Kearns as quoted in Boyett and Conn, *Workplace 2000*, p. 9.

4. Karl Albrecht, *At America's Service* (New York: Warner Books, 1992).

5. Hal Morgan and Kerry Tucker, *Companies That Care* (New York: Fireside, 1991).

# CHAPTER TEN

# Workplace Ethics in a World Setting

Moral dilemmas faced by businesses at home are faced on a larger scale by businesses that span the globe. This is especially true when cultural and economic differences between countries are great. While what we address applies to our practices as Americas in the global economy, we believe these comments can be applied as well to how others are treated and respond to us in our country. A universal need for common understanding about what is and is not ethical practice will become a larger part of the agenda of commerce in the future.

## BRIBERY AND GIFT GIVING

A company that does not respect the people in its host country will probably not stay there for long. Worker morale, the cooperation of local governments, local people's enthusiasm for buying a company's products—all are jeopardized when the host country is not respected. Respect requires sensitivity to that country's customs and culture, as well as an ethical philosophy that guides the international goals of the company. Respect can be undermined by a number of different business practices that occur all too frequently; probably the worst of them is offering bribes to government officials.

In a typical case, a marketing team visiting a developing country for the first time hears that they need to offer bribes to government officials in order to do business there. The stories may be untrue or exaggerations. If the company is inclined to believe the worst, the stories become self-fulfilling prophecies and great harm is done to the business climate in the new country. An understanding of the potential for honest business transactions in the developing country may be lost because American business people assumed the worst.

But what if bribery *is* an "expected business practice" in a particular foreign country? An American corporation planning to open a factory there does have good reason to believe that export licenses go only to those who pay the biggest bribes.

The moral answer: The company should refuse to cooperate even if this means cancelation of the new operation. The company should accept temporary defeat. It should not pay the bribe, both because doing so is illegal under the Foreign Corrupt Practices Act of 1977 and because the practice of bribery is morally wrong. The moral answer does not accept the argument that American companies should "adapt themselves to local customs" when the customs include bribery. Even if it were true that "everyone is doing it," that would not make bribery right. We give away something fundamental and irretrievable when we conduct our affairs according to someone else's view of right and wrong.

Consider now a different viewpoint. Suppose that an American company has been legally exporting its products from Country X, but is suddenly told that its export license will not be renewed unless a bribe is paid. The company will suffer large financial losses if it cannot fulfill its contracts. In a case such as this, we do not want to say that bribery could never be justified as the least of evils after the company had determined that no other option was available. A company has to look after the interests of stockholders, consumers, and employees. Under such circumstances, bribery becomes economic blackmail, and each company must determine how best to get its products and ultimately itself out of such an environment. Nevertheless, once a company agrees to pay under duress, it becomes known as a corporation that *can* be coerced, and this increases the likelihood that it and other companies will be coerced in the future. As a general rule, it is far better not to give in to such pressures in the first place.

If bribery is wrong, then what about practices that appear to resemble bribery, such as the custom of giving and accepting gifts when engaging in business transactions? The gifts may be quite expensive. Such gift giving is common in many foreign countries and occurs as well in our own country.

It may be morally and legally permissible for Americans to go along with this practice. Gift giving is not the same as bribery when it is a part of "normal" business expenses or business etiquette. By means of gift giving, someone's value or dignity or standing may be recognized. It can be a way of saying "thank you" when it occurs at the end of a successful transaction.

The Japanese custom of exchanging gifts is widely practiced and pertains both to those who do not actually obtain contracts and to those who do obtain contracts. A number of different individuals may receive gifts in the course of a single business transaction. Gift giving can, most of the time, be seen as more like tipping in a restaurant. It is often an expensive and elaborate part of the process, however, and can get out of hand. Part of what is required for an American to understand a foreign country is a willingness to go along with practices that we Americans may not feel comfortable with—as long as the practices are not strongly objectionable.

In contrast to the majority of gift-giving expectations, it is part of the definition of bribery that the payment *not* be a normal expense incurred to engage in the business at hand. Bribes are usually given to ensure that *you* get the permit or contract while someone else who did not offer a bribe or as large a bribe will not get the permit or contract. Paying a bribe replaces market criteria for deciding among competitors. It undermines the common good, which is better served through competitive processes, and it is a direct assault on individual rights.

We do not mean to imply that the custom of gift giving is not potentially corrupting, but only that it is not essentially so—not bad through and through—the way bribery is. The custom of gift giving offers great potential for favoritism and conflicts of interest; it ought to be scrutinized and resisted whenever and wherever possible. Perhaps ideally, the practice of giving gifts to facilitate business transactions should be "nudged" toward extinction, but it can be and often is used with sensitivity and builds goodwill.

To return to a discussion of bribery: Not only is it a direct assault on market mechanisms for allocating contracts in business, but it is pernicious also at a deeper level. Bribing public officials may help to keep them in office; if these same officials use their positions of power to make themselves richer at public expense, they may do incalculable harm to their own people as well as to foreign interests. The more that public officials rely upon bribes, whether from people in their own country or from foreigners, the less they need to rely upon popular support. Some of the foreign governments that Ameri-

can corporations have helped to keep in power eventually threatened the interests of these corporations, all the while exploiting their
own citizens. Bad governments do harm in countless ways, dragging
everyone down.

The Foreign Corrupt Practices Act recognizes an important distinction between relatively large payments to people high in government, for the presumed purpose of influencing their decisions, and
smaller payments to lesser officials who do not have the same decision-making powers. The latter are treated more leniently; they
include the sorts of "gift giving" and more routine payments for various
purposes that we have discussed above. The Foreign Corrupt Practices Act has been much criticized, but we believe that it is essentially sound, a positive legacy of the Carter administration. American views of what is corrupt may well change, however, and new
legislation is bound to be written. Keeping up with legislation that
helps to define what is and is not acceptable practice in foreign countries
is part of the responsibility we each have when working outside the
United States.

## POLITICAL INVOLVEMENT IN FOREIGN COUNTRIES

Should a multinational corporation involve itself in the election process in a host country? Some writers on ethics say flatly that
a hands-off policy ought to be followed, because corporations have
a vested interest in the results. They seem to think that the mere
existence of a potential conflict of interest justifies a hands-off policy.
Such a view may be too extreme. Still, the interests of a foreign
corporation may well be at odds with the interests of the host country, and foreign business people may be tempted at election time to
finance their favored candidates on this basis. Such efforts, which
are a form of bribery, will almost surely backfire in the long run
when the citizens of the country realize the corporation has sold
them out. Goodwill lost when multinational corporations support
corrupt governments is irreplaceable.

At best, political involvement in a host country by foreign
businesses is risky, in part because it is difficult to predict how elected
officials will behave and because foreign understanding of the issues in local elections may be unclear and biased by economic issues. Such involvement may be misperceived and unappreciated by
the citizens of the host country as well. Working publicly to improve

the political atmosphere without private involvement in the process is a strategy that seems both ethically and culturally sensitive. Whatever involvement a company might take must be of such a nature that the involvement can be known.

## LAW VS. MORALITY

For corporate managers—at home or abroad—to say in defense of their policies that they have adhered to the letter of the law is never in itself sufficient. There will always be cases where laws and regulations are inadequate. As we have said throughout this book, the pursuit of profit within the law must be tempered by other values. This is all the more true when corporations do business in developing countries whose legal systems do little to curb pollution, eliminate unsafe work conditions, or prevent the sale of products that pose health risks. This raises the question: Do American companies have a moral obligation to adhere to American legal standards when doing business in foreign countries?

Our general answer to this question is no. American laws and regulations are not in themselves moral rules. Morality sometimes means going beyond laws, as we have said. Substituting American laws for those in another country will not automatically produce morality; that would be both too easy and too difficult. It would be too easy because it would relieve American corporations of the need to wrestle with moral dilemmas themselves. They could say: "We have followed all of the legal standards that apply in the United States, so we must be doing the right thing." In reality, in some instances they ought to be doing more than the American legal standards require.

At the same time, American standards may be difficult to implement in foreign countries because of the levels of industrialization and the availability of resources in those countries. Consider, for example, the U.S. Food and Drug Administration (FDA) regulations. There are a number of reasons why they may be difficult to implement in a developing nation:

- Countries that are poorer than the United States may not be able to afford the "Cadillac" standards mandated here relative to needs in the developing country.
- Like all regulatory policies, FDA regulations have been estab-

lished in response to a variety of different pressures, some of them essentially political. Hence, the regulations are compromises and not necessarily best even for the United States.

• Beyond economic and political differences, there will be other important differences between the United States and a particular developing country. For example, the incidence of a particular disease could be markedly different, affecting the urgency and priority in marketing a new medicine.

Multinational pharmaceutical companies are left with a difficult task in their efforts to distinguish between what is ethical and what is unethical. They may well be left with a greater temptation to cut corners in their business dealings in foreign countries than in the United States—a temptation that is augmented by the fact that consumers in developing countries are less sophisticated on the whole than consumers at home. Some foreign consumers are not even able to read the instructions on the package. This was part of the problem that led to the scandals in the 1970s involving foreign sales of infant formula; babies got sick and many died because illiterate mothers could not follow the directions written in their own language.

Consumers in developing countries are usually not able to carry out comparison shopping to the degree possible in the United States. Multinational corporations thus have all the more responsibility to implement a positive vision of their corporate mission that embraces the best interests of customers, suppliers, workers, and the host country over the longer term.

However, the moral injunction "Do what is best for all concerned" is not going to be particularly helpful, especially in a multinational corporation whose governance is split among executives, boards of directors, and investors. Every multinational corporation is faced with strong actual and potential competition from all around the world. What can be done to make it easier for multinational corporations, such as pharmaceutical companies, to conduct themselves in an ethical manner?

## INDUSTRY-WIDE MORAL CODES

The most important avenue for corporations to follow is to make strong efforts toward developing industry-wide moral codes that they and their competitors adhere to voluntarily. If an international group such as the World Health Organization develops reasonable standards, as happened in the wake of the infant formula marketing scandals, then corporations should support these organizations and urge other companies to do likewise. Industry-wide standards provide essential benchmarks.

The more industry-wide and world-wide standards are taken seriously, the more competing companies are put in the same camp regarding product safety and performance, employee working conditions, resource use, etc. Fewer opportunities will exist for individual companies to exploit people in developing countries. Also, when standards transcend the policies of a single company, those who follow the standards are less likely to receive criticism from other sources.

Nevertheless, even where industry-wide standards have been established, there is no substitute for *understanding the people and the culture that a corporation does business with.* How is such understanding to be achieved?

## PUTTING ONESELF IN THE SHOES OF ANOTHER

A good place to begin is with application of the "Reversibility of Roles" test, the basic idea for which is contained in the Golden Rule. The requirement is to "put yourself in the shoes" of all interested parties prior to making any moral decision. Critics have always asked: Is it possible to reverse roles in the way required? Can I genuinely place myself in the cultural and ideological shoes of all the other parties?

To reverse roles with employees, customers, and suppliers in foreign countries, managers of multinational corporations can begin by asking themselves pertinent questions. What follows are illustrative examples only; many similar questions can and should be asked:

- If I lived in a country without democratic government, would I want that government to be kept in power by foreign corporations that bribe public officials?
- Would I want a multinational corporation to operate in my country with its only concern being to make as much money as quickly as it could?

- If I lived in a country with an unstable government, would I want a foreign corporation, acting in what it took to be its own interest, to undermine efforts toward political reform?
- How would I feel if a foreign corporation bought extensive agricultural holdings to raise crops for export, increasing malnutrition in the host country because the remaining agricultural land was inadequate to supply the local market?

The existence of multinational corporations teaches dramatically the moral requirement for everyone to "walk a mile in the other person's shoes." This lesson, writ large on the world scene, applies also to the operations of businesses at home. We hope that the education of business people that results from their experiences abroad will be a two-way street—lessons learned at home will be applied abroad, and lessons learned or relearned abroad will be applied at home.

## GENDER ISSUES

We have as yet said nothing in this chapter about gender-related moral questions. They arise frequently when American companies do business in countries where women are treated very differently from in the United States. Should Americans in Saudi Arabia, for example, adhere to Saudi attitudes toward women? Our answer to this question is both yes and no. Our reason for hesitation—for not flatly opposing sexist practices wherever they occur—is *not* that we believe in the "cultural relativity" of women's rights, any more than we believe in the cultural relativity of bribery. Nevertheless, bribery and sexual discrimination need to be treated in somewhat different ways.

One important difference has to do with how the two practices are perceived by people in the foreign countries where Americans do business. In those cultures that do not recognize the equality of men and women, there is likely to be a widespread, culture-based understanding of the "proper role of women." It will be shared by a much larger segment of the population than is the acceptance of bribery in *any* country. In Saudi Arabia sexual discrimination pervades virtually all aspects of life, but bribery is not official policy. Even in cultures where bribery is widely practiced, people do not judge it to be morally correct in the way that sexual discrimination is judged to be morally correct.

Why is this so? Presumably, the reason is that bribery is not consistent with standards for honesty and truth-telling that lie at so deep a level that virtually every culture must accept them. Regrettably, a belief in the absolute and total equality of men and women does not lie at so deep a level. Often, the roles of men and women follow the prescriptions of religion and are held as sacred, as is our belief in equality of opportunity.

Still, it might be argued that sexual equality *is* as important as truth-telling. We agree. However, another moral value exists that has equal standing with the two just mentioned: Respect for human beings in all their cultural diversity, regardless of whether or not they share the values that we hold dear. Americans living or doing business abroad must both respect people who belong to other cultures *and* stick to their convictions in regard to women's rights. The only way to do both of these things is to engage in what we would like to call "progressive compromise."

Progressive compromise calls for an American company in Saudi Arabia, for example, to slow down somewhat on the implementation of its commitment to gender equality, but in a way that does not mask or deny faith in that concept. For example, the company *should* assign women executives to its Saudi branch, but it should not parade them in front of Saudi executives and officials. It should make their competence known but keep their presence subdued. When it comes to hiring local people, the company should attempt to strike a balance between the standards of the host country and the company's own standards.

The policy we are advocating is an example of the same "moral nudging" that we urged upon salespeople in Chapter Four. We said that the basic moral requirement is taking action that will improve the situation in an area of business that traditionally has fallen short of strict adherence to the highest moral norms—to become better, not perfect. An absolute requirement in this delicate area of ethical decision-making lies in the process, not in a particular outcome. That is the basic requirement for incremental change.

Change in gender attitudes and relationships is without question coming to all of the world's countries; we hope that American corporations will play their part in helping to set the direction for change.

## RAW MATERIALS

Some have argued that it is morally wrong for multinationals to set up operations in developing nations for the sole purpose of exporting raw materials from those countries. Such a practice amounts to exploitation, critics say, because each country has a right to the development of its own materials, for its own people. Otherwise, the country becomes simply a supply depot for richer countries: Its oil, gas, timber, and ores go to support the living standards of people in richer countries while those in the developing country are left with nothing.

There is nothing fundamentally wrong with the establishment of a business whose sole purpose is the exportation of raw materials from a developing nation. A country has the right to sell some of its natural resources if it chooses to do so. Different countries have different economic strengths and weaknesses. Some can do better selling finished products, while others are more effective when they focus on, as examples, mining or the timber industry, neither of which has to be exploitative.

However, both the mining industry and the timber industry can easily become exploitative. When resources are taken from a developing country, the questions we want answered first are these:

1. Who possesses legal title to those resources?
2. Are the people who have titles to land and resources the ones who "really" own them, or ought to own them?
3. Who gets the money paid for resources by the multinational corporation?
4. What policy exists for the replacement of resources where this is possible, as in the timber industry?

In the worst cases, multinationals are guilty of receiving stolen property, because the politicians who sell the resources have no right to them. Even if these politicians do have a "legal" right to the resources, the fact that a business transaction involves no bribes or coercion is no guarantee that it is moral. Land and resources can be controlled by a corrupt government or by individuals who have acquired the land or resources through corrupt actions. For example, some countries exclude certain classes of people from ownership of resources, keeping these people forever in the debt of a "landed class" or other privileged group.

Here as elsewhere, one essential moral test is whether or not individuals or corporations have in their business transactions taken into account the best interests of all the people in the country involved. Achieving morality in managing natural resources is perhaps more difficult than in any other area of business.

On the positive side, when resources are sold on the world market, a developing country should certainly receive currency that it badly needs.

On the negative side, because the economy of the exporting country is by definition (as a developing nation) in its early stages, the market price of the resources will almost surely not reflect the value that these resources will acquire once the economy of the nation has developed—once the country can afford to develop its own resources. But by that time it may be too late. The resources may be gone and the opportunity for the people of the country to become players in international competition may be lost or significantly diminished.

What can be done to help safeguard the developing country? Leaving aside the few instances where philanthropy may play a significant role, the best safeguard may reside in a *genuinely* competitive market worldwide and stable reinvestment strategies in the host country. Competitive market forces can help preserve resources by allowing investors *in* the developing country to take a longer term view of the resources they control—the interactive nature of the use of natural resources and the potential to maintain their value over time through careful development.

"Market forces" will not operate in this way—they will operate in exactly the opposite way, in fact—if the resources are controlled by a corrupt individual or if the political situation is so unstable that no long-term investments seem safe. Both of these circumstances lead to an attitude of "take the money and run," which is disastrous for the people of the developing country.

What can a multinational do here in the interest of morality? It can refuse to deal with corrupt governments, whether by buying resources from them or by paying them bribes. It can support political reform toward more democratic governments, as we mentioned earlier, and it can support government policies that strengthen market conditions. *It can refuse to take advantage of special treatment that it would not receive in an genuinely open market.* It can seek out honorable people in a host country with whom to have business dealings. It can support land reform. It can work toward extending industry-wide codes of conduct to include strict guidelines for the acquisition and development of natural resources. It can make its dealings with foreign countries open to public review.

## HEALTH AND SAFETY

Industry-wide codes can be especially effective for improving workplace conditions, as for example in foreign mines. In past years, some multinationals have been guilty of gross moral violations in the treatment of foreign miners; some companies and their countries are still reaping the consequences of ill will generated decades ago. American Occupational Safety and Health Administration (OSHA) standards or their equivalents cannot be applied automatically in foreign countries. However, a company that knowingly supports health-endangering practices is acting unethically. We urge a continuing moral commitment by all multinational corporations to treat employees at home and abroad with respect.

Financial success in any area of business can be achieved at too great a cost. We have said this before. Nowhere is it more true than in the treatment of employees at the bottom of the employment ladder and in hazardous jobs in foreign countries where far too little may be done to protect workers.

# CHAPTER ELEVEN

# Implications for Action

Much advice has been offered in this book, but the impetus for real change lies outside its pages. It lies with all of the individuals who take part in the world of business. When and if a sufficient number of them decide that it is time to transform their companies along lines similar to those outlined in this book, the workplace will become more ethical and better able to produce high-quality goods and services.

Each of you must determine the initial steps to take in your own workplace situation: the questions to be asked; the advice that should be sought or given; changes that are called for in office settings, assignments, or larger scale workplace expectations; needed adjustments to your own perceptions and attitudes; and skills that you may want to acquire. In determining your role and your starting point in initiating change, look first at yourself as an individual, and second at your position in the company that employs you. Everyone, regardless of job description, can make an important difference. However, senior managers bear the largest responsibility—to determine where and when an organizational response is needed in regard to structures, policies, and procedures.

This book is perhaps more difficult to summarize than many because it combines ideas from three quite different fields—moral philosophy, business management, and behavioral psychology. The points that follow are not offered as summary statements, but rather, as parting thoughts that we hope will help you in choosing your own path. The first three are directed to everyone in the workplace. So is the last point. Those numbered 4 through 9 are directed primarily to managers.

*EACH INDIVIDUAL*:

*1. Support the idea that ethical behavior is always possible in business.*

Whenever you encounter someone whose words or deeds indicate that he or she believes business activity to be amoral, respond. Take a stand that is sensitive yet direct.

Talk that perpetuates the view that business is amoral is cheap, easy, and frequently encountered. People who are cynical, believe themselves to be "worldly wise," or are sincere and thoughtful but simply mistaken, seem to find talk about the "amorality of business" as effortless as breathing. Like bad currency that drives out good, such talk sabotages efforts to present the other side.

The primary point to get across is that the world of business is all of a piece with other aspects of life and therefore should not play by any special set of rules. Honesty, kindness, concern for society as a whole and for future generations, a healthy feeling of self-worth, and respect for the rights of others—these values belong as much in the business world as elsewhere. The pursuit of profit in business is fine and necessary—if tempered by these values.

*2. Reach people at their own level.*

Your role in maintaining or changing other people's actions can be active or passive. If you choose to do nothing when you observe harmful words or actions, you are most probably weighing the "safety" of inaction against the varied costs of involvement. We want to encourage you to speak up, but from a perspective that endorses other people's ability to change and that lends support to the idea that increased skill in doing the right thing can be learned.

For example, there are people who rarely if ever hear the words "ethical" or "integrity" applied to what they say or do. They may pride themselves on their tough, "real world" posture. To catch such people doing something right for its own sake and to point it out in appropriate terms may cause them to begin to see new possibilities. While their new insight may not bring about a permanent change in behavior, helping them to achieve the insight is nevertheless a kind and ethical act on your part.

Endorsing the specific acts of a person does not mean endorsing the totality of a person's actions. Allow a generous and forgiving spirit to guide you in dealing with the selfish among us, while staying clear of involvements that use or abuse you or that increase an individual's "success" in behaving badly. We should all hope that in our moments of selfishness, someone else will help us be better than we are.

*3. Do not become discouraged if you sometimes feel that you are the only employee in your company who takes ethics seriously.*

An important thought to keep in mind: The "business ethics revolution" has only just begun, two decades at most having passed since its inception. Revolutions are rarely instantaneous. The majority of business managers who are presently in positions of influence did not take a business ethics course in college, and they passed through their formative years at a time when prevailing attitudes were quite different from what they are now. The "quality movement" is an even more recent phenomenon in the United States. Similarly, the impetus from psychology to eliminate coercive management styles is in a fledgling stage. So don't abandon the cause.

In a few years, many others will catch up with you. A thoroughgoing commitment to the ethical treatment of everyone in business (and outside of it) is the wave of the future.

*MANAGERS:*

*4. Develop a public ethical code that promotes individual choice and responsibility as well as corporate requirements.*

Business can become its own best policy setter, its own best overseer in ethical matters. Certain groups have begun in earnest to carve out industry standards for ethical practices in their fields. Each business can do the same inside its own operation as well. Whenever possible, establish the expectation that individuals will evaluate and make decisions according to ethical standards.

*5. Select and retain ethical employees.*

Make sure right from the point of an employee's entry into the company that you have examined that person's ethical commitments. As thoroughly as possible, examine not only what prospective employees say they have done when faced with ethical dilemmas, but what they have actually done. Sometimes references can help to validate character—personal integrity, a respect for rights, a commitment to justice, and a desire to make society a better place. The business person who is willing to cut ethical corners for the sake of profits may be tough and competent, but you should set up barriers to that person's entry into your company.

In order to avoid hiring the wrong people in the first place, evaluate what prospective employees might mean by expressions such as "treating others with respect" and "following through on commitments." Further, ensure that these phrases and others that point to an awareness of ethical obligations are contained in job specifications. At the present time in the business world, the characteristics described by these phrases are frequently viewed as merely incidental to the interview process, not as the stuff of tough-minded interviews. They should be assigned an importance equal to the technical requirements for a job. In any event, if you are looking for certain personal qualities in your employees, you must plan your interviews and ask questions accordingly.

*6. Make ethical behavior part of performance review.*

The large majority of individuals in business are ethical. Most people desire to do the right thing. But some people have learned other ways of acting, ways that put short-term and selfish goals foremost. Some people are or become insensitive to the needs of others. Labeling any of these people as "unethical" will almost surely prove to be counterproductive. Instead, you have an obligation to examine what you can do at a reasonable cost to yourself and your company to change their behavior. You may have no choice but to remove such individuals from the company, but that is not usually the case. As long as they remain working at their jobs, you can assign them performance goals that compete with their usual styles of behavior.

For example, someone who does not demonstrate respect for others can learn new ways of acting by being placed in situations that require cooperation and trust, and the give and take of working with others. Set up working conditions that require reliance on others wherever possible. Give these individuals a chance to modify their behavior through well-designed processes of change. Assess them accordingly.

*7. Work on increasing moral sensitivity from as many different perspectives as possible.*

Do not allow your work environment to be one that pushes the tough issues of business decisions under a mountain of numbers, technical demands, or marketplace surveys. Encourage people to look at the numbers in a budget reduction plan in terms of human costs. This will not make the decisions bad ones, but rather will provide a solid guidepost against which individuals can measure the true costs of decisions. It will help to ensure that decision-makers are not removed—by walls, management hierarchies, or board room meetings—from the realities of the situation.

Bring ethics into your employees' work day by discussing the issues faced by laid-off workers, disappointed customers, family members of employees transferred at short notice, mothers with young children who are not permitted flexible work hours, older employees who are still competent and capable of a full day's work if they are not rushed or intimidated, handicapped individuals who could become valuable employees in work environments that are suitably modified, and so on.

The natural extension of this idea is for companies to initiate "ethics sensitivity workshops." Depending on your role in the organization, it may be appropriate for you to conduct such workshops yourself after receiving training that would contribute to your own moral sensitivity and professional development. Or you may want to consider bringing in professionals to do the job.

*8. Make ethics a fundamental part of workplace expectations.*

If people in the workplace are rewarded for behaving more ethically, then they will behave more ethically—and their attitudes and beliefs will likely change as well. They will have been taught ethics in the fullest sense. Moral leadership, the day-to-day pressures and influences of the workplace, examples set by managers and co-workers, statements of corporate values, "vision" statements, the culture of a corporation—all can help in making people more ethical.

*9. Attach consequences to desired behavior, measure its occurrence, and change your activities as needed to maintain ethical actions.*

As we have emphasized, it is not enough merely to expect the

right performance. A company through its managers must design the
motivational incentives to produce the behavior desired.

*EVERYONE:*

*10. Follow the decision-making model of moral pluralism outlined
in Chapter Five.*
    In all that you do, whether as an individual or as a manager
representing a business, evaluate your actions against achieving a
balance among the basic values of rights, justice, the common good,
and self-interest.

# Index

# About the Authors

**Ralph W. Clark,** a professor of philosophy at West Virginia University, teaches courses in business ethics, current moral problems, and ethical theory. He has published in such journals as *Philosophy*, *The Monist*, *The Journal of Value Inquiry*, and *Philosophical Studies*. His other books are *Introduction to Moral Reasoning* and *Introduction to Philosophical Thinking*.

**Alice Darnell Lattal** is an organizational and management consultant to companies across America. She has a doctorate in clinical psychology and is employed by Corporate Behavior Analysts, Inc. She works with companies facing change, often examining what managements say they want in their products, services, and culture, and what the policies, procedures, and practices actually produce. She has taught at the university level, published in professional journals, and written on ethics in *Behaviorism and Ethics*.